Tales for Transforming Adversity

Tales for Transforming Adversity

A Buddhist Lama's Advice for Life's Ups and Downs

Khenpo Sodargye

Wisdom Publications
199 Elm Street
Somerville, MA 02144 USA
wisdompubs.org

Library of Congress Cataloging-in-Publication Data
Names: Suodaji, Kanbu, 1962– author.
Title: Tales for transforming adversity: a Buddhist Lama's advice for life's ups
    and downs / Khenpo Sodargye.
Description: Somerville, MA: Wisdom Publications, 2017. |
Identifiers: LCCN 2017005564 (print) | LCCN 2017028532 (ebook) | ISBN
    9781614292708 (ebook) | ISBN 1614292701 (ebook) | ISBN 9781614292555
    (pbk.: alk. paper) | ISBN 1614292558 (pbk.: alk. paper)
Subjects: LCSH: Suffering—Religious aspects—Buddhism. | Life—Religious
    aspects—Buddhism.
Classification: LCC BQ4235 (ebook) | LCC BQ4235 .S86 2017 (print) | DDC
    294.3/4442—dc23
LC record available at https://lccn.loc.gov/2017005564

ISBN 978-1-61429-255-5   ebook ISBN 978-1-61429-270-8

21 20 19 18 17   5 4 3 2

Translated by Ke Jiang. Cover design by Phil Pascuzzo.
Set in Jannon 10 Pro 10/15.

Contents

CONTENTS

Preface

How often do we feel satisfied with our life? Ancient sages say that if we divide our life into ten equal parts, we are only happy for one or two of them. The Buddha, too, reminds us again and again that life is riddled with suffering. Even setting aside the suffering of birth, old age, sickness, and death, it's impossible to avoid the suffering of being separated from loved ones, encountering enemies, and generally not getting what we want.

Some people might object, saying, "There's obviously a lot of joy in life. Why does the Buddha emphasize suffering?" While Buddhism certainly recognizes suffering, it doesn't deny that there is happiness in life, too. The problem with this happiness is that it's fragile and fleeting. Happiness tints our life, but it's not the primary hue. The only certainty in life is that everything changes. The powerful can become prisoners, devoted friends can become enemies, happy families can split, and even people who live for a long time will eventually die. Indeed, even the best circumstances change, and change causes suffering. This is what we mean when we say that life is full of suffering. If you refuse to recognize this, insisting that life is a joyride, blinding yourself to reality, and mistaking suffering for happiness, then you lose your chance to be *truly* free from suffering. Facing the truth of suffering is the first step toward real and lasting happiness. The Buddha became awakened only after first witnessing the suffering of old age, sickness, and death. So don't try to avoid suffering, and don't be afraid of it.

Some people only want comfort and are unwilling to face the suffering that lies in store for them. This is simply unrealistic. Life is full of rainstorms and bumpy rides, and besides, without the wind, frost, snow, and rain, there would be no blossoms in the spring or fruit in the fall. Also, a lot of people believe that altruism—seeking the happiness of others—brings no reward, not realizing that, on the contrary, it's the most rewarding thing there is. They think that accepting the truth of impermanence will reduce their drive and ambition, not realizing that living with the truth of change makes life more fascinating. Instead, they spend their time worrying about their possessions and their reputation. Unfortunately, none of these will ensure a peaceful death, let alone happiness in future lives. We need to become masters of our own mind. No matter how complicated the situation might be, or how unbearable life feels, the best medicine for living well is practicing what the Buddha taught.

When I wrote *Tales for Transforming Adversity*, my target readers were people living in Han Chinese areas, because I have known and understood their lives and suffering quite well. To my surprise, the book was embraced widely; many people found approaches to tame their minds through these ancient and contemporary stories from both the East and West. Moreover, since simple stories can leave a deep impression, it is easy to recollect them in challenging or difficult times, so readers found the messages in this book useful in their everyday lives.

But the anxieties and questions addressed in this book are not Chinese problems or Tibetan problems. They are human problems, gnawing at people of all different colors, speaking different languages, in every corner of the world. I am delighted that through the efforts of many, this English version has finally come into being and may be able to bring ease and happiness to many more people in this turbulent age.

Khenpo Sodargye
Larung Gar Buddhist Institute, 2017

1

How Can We Live without Suffering?

A life without hardship is like an empty ship,
easily overturned in a storm.

Strengths and Weaknesses

Everyone has strengths and weaknesses. Even the greatest among us have shortcomings, and those limited in their capacities have strengths. There's no point in comparing your shortcomings with the virtues of others. Those others might believe they could never match you in certain ways. The Daoist philosopher Zhuangzi's "Autumn Floods" says:

> The one-footed yak wished it were a millipede because a millipede can walk. The millipede wished it were a snake because a snake can slither very fast. The snake wished it were the wind because the wind can move even faster. The wind wished it were as swift as eyesight. Eyesight, however, wished it were the mind, since the mind can move in less than an instant.

Buddhist scriptures say that the mind is the swiftest of all things. The point is that, when comparing yourself with others, since there's always someone better than you at something, don't be overly inflated, and since even the greatest have weaknesses, don't be overly self-critical. As it is said, "A foot has its shortness; an inch has its length."

A fable illustrates this. Once, a little mouse wanted dearly to be strong and brave. Looking up at the sky one day, the mouse was struck by its vastness and thought that the sky must be the strongest thing that there was. It called out, "Sky, you must not be afraid of anything. I'm so very small. Could you help me be strong and brave?"

The sky replied, "I am afraid of some things. I'm afraid of dark clouds. When they cover me up, I can't see anything."

So the little mouse concluded that dark clouds were even stronger than the sky. It found a dark cloud and said to it, "Cloud, you can cover the sky and block out the sun. You must be the strongest thing in the world. You must not be afraid of anything. I'm so very small. Could you help me be strong and brave?"

The dark cloud said, "I am afraid of strong winds. I work hard to cover the sky, but when the wind comes, I'm blown away."

So the little mouse went to the wind with the same question. The wind answered, "I am afraid of walls. I can't go through them, so walls are stronger than me."

So then, of course, the little mouse went to see a wall and asked, "Wall, you can stop the wind. Are you the strongest thing in the world?"

The wall's answer stunned him: "Not at all. What I'm most afraid of are mice! They can make holes in me, and enough of those can make me collapse."

The little mouse rolled over in astonishment. "I've looked everywhere, searching the world for the strongest thing, but it turns out that actually it is me!"

It is a mistake to look at the strengths of others and conclude that we're worthless. Often we don't realize how powerful we are.

If You Seek the Wrong Thing, Misery Follows

All things are impermanent. Everything, including our body, wealth, reputation, and relationships, will change. We also don't keep these things when we die. Only our mind stays with us through life and death.

Long ago there was a merchant who had four wives. He was very fond of his fourth wife and would do whatever she asked. He had struggled to win the heart of his third wife, so he always kept her with him and spoke sweetly to her. His second wife was his confidante, and he spoke to her every day. His first wife was like a maid, following his every word without complaint, but she didn't have a real place in his heart.

Once, the merchant was preparing for a long trip and asked each of his wives if they would go with him.

The fourth wife simply refused to go.

The third wife said, "If even your favorite wife won't go, why should I?"

The second wife said, "I'll see you off, but I don't want to go someplace far away."

Only the first wife said, "Wherever you go and however far it is, I'm happy to go!"

What does this mean? His fourth and favorite wife represents the body. While we are alive, we see it as the most important thing we have, but at the time of death, it won't go with us. The third wife represents our wealth. No matter how hard we work to get it, at the time of death we can't even take a penny. The second wife represents our friends and relatives. When we die, at best they shed some tears and bury us. The first wife represents our mind. It's the closest thing to us but also the most easily neglected, since we would rather invest all our energy in external things.

This is why a master once said, "We have so many strange ideas: we can't wait to grow up, but then we lament our long-lost childhood. We make ourselves ill earning money, but then we spend it all on getting better. Death always seems a long way off, but when we die, it seems as if life was too short. We constantly worry about the future and ignore the happiness of the present moment."

If we understand that all things change—they come into being when conditions arise and come to an end when conditions cease—then even what we have right now will seem marvelous. We will stop madly pursuing fame and worldly gain, and when misfortunes plague us, we won't fall into desperation. In short, if we get used to change and accept it, it will prevent us from blaming others for our problems and let us relax our bodies and open our minds.

Optimism and Pessimism

Not long ago, a lay student of mine gave me a call and said, "Khenpo, I've been listless and depressed recently and have been thinking that a change of scenery might do me good." This reminded me of a story.

Once, a man had two sons and decided to call them Optimist and Pessimist. These two children grew up in the same environment but had very different personalities. Optimist was always happy no matter what problems he ran into, whereas Pessimist always felt oppressed even when everything was going well.

At some point, the man regretted having given such ridiculous names to his sons. To try to somehow reverse the process, he decided to leave Optimist on a pile of manure and Pessimist on a heap of jewels and toys. After a while, the man went back to see what had happened. To his surprise, Optimist was enjoying himself exploring the dung heap and told him, "You asked me to stay here, so there must be a treasure in here somewhere!" Pessimist, on the other hand, was sitting sadly in the middle of all the jewels and had smashed half of the toys. When he saw this, their father realized that in order to change your mood, it's not enough to change the circumstances.

All of our experiences are projections of our own minds. Due to different mental states, our perspectives on the same objects can be worlds apart. That's why it is said that when a pessimist sees a rose bush, he will complain about the thorns, whereas an optimist will appreciate the flowers. We can try a change of scenery, but far more powerful is to change our mind.

Whether our life is happy or miserable isn't determined primarily by external conditions. The American essayist Ralph Waldo Emerson wrote,

"The pleasure of life is according to the man that lives it, and not according to the work or the place." Many things in your life won't go as planned. If you can't face problems directly, blaming things on others and trying to find happiness by changing your external conditions, then you'll make yourself miserable. No matter what situation you're in or how much frustration you feel, it's better to tame your mind than to blame the circumstances. That works better than anything!

Suffering and Happiness Are
the Work of the Mind

I was chatting recently with a very good friend. We talked about many things, from Dharma to daily life, engrossed in pleasant conversation. Suddenly it was time for lunch, and someone brought us each a bowl of noodles. As soon as I saw it, my mouth started watering, and when I tasted it, it was fantastic. It had never occurred to me that meeting a good friend could make food taste so good. The power of the mind really is incredible.

I remember when I was just a little boy, my father took me to Trango. On the way, we passed through a small town called Drimdu. We had a bowl of noodles in a little noodle shack. Even now, several decades later, I still remember how good those noodles were. Since then I've tasted a lot of famous delicacies, but none of them has ever matched the flavor of that bowl of noodles. Of course, I know very well that the noodles in such a small town couldn't have been that extraordinary, but everything is affected by our moods. I could have been especially delighted because back then it would have been a rare chance for me to eat out or because in those days there wasn't a lot of good food to be had.

One fable gives a similar illustration. Once, an exiled emperor tasted some particularly good tofu. It was so delicious that he thought it must be as good as ambrosia in heaven. When he returned to the palace after his exile, he commanded many great chefs to reproduce this tofu. No matter how skilled they were or how much they tried, the tofu never tasted as good. His attachment to that flavor was so extreme that he had chefs who failed beheaded. Had he understood the meaning of "the object is the work of the mind," he would never have gone that far! Unfortunately, very few people in this world understand the relation between the mind and the external world.

Self-Reliance

If you're successful and carefree thanks only to the support of others, your luck may run out. Some people only manage to obtain good jobs and so forth through family connections. However, since their parents' positions may change, and since their parents will eventually die, there's no certainty that such fortunes will last. It's best to rely on yourself.

There's an ancient story about two swans and a turtle who lived together in a pond. One summer there was a severe drought. Seeing their pond about to dry up, they became restless like cats on hot bricks. One of the swans said, "We shouldn't wait here to die; we should fly to the far-away lake." The turtle was upset at the prospect of being deserted. The swans said, "We can fly, but you can't. What can we do?"

The turtle had an idea: "If each of you hold one end of a stick, I can bite it in the middle, and then we can all fly together." The two swans thought it was a good idea and agreed. They picked up the turtle and began the long flight toward the far-away lake.

As they flew they passed over a village, and some children saw them. The children clapped their hands and called out, "What clever swans, making a turtle fly!" The turtle was annoyed and thought, "This flying idea was mine! Why should the swans get the credit?!" Although the turtle wanted to say something, he didn't want to fall, so he swallowed his pride and kept quiet.

A little while later they passed another village, and another group of children saw them and also called out, applauding the swans. This time the turtle couldn't restrain himself and shouted, "It was my idea!" Of course, as soon as he opened his mouth, he fell to the ground and died.

People who are careless and boastful while depending on others for their good fortune will eventually fall. If others treat you with kindness, recognize this and be appreciative—not like this turtle!

People who depend on others for their survival will, just like this turtle, eventually suffer. Therefore be grateful for the help you receive, but put effort into enhancing your own abilities rather than relying too much on the generosity of others. The ancients said, "The scholars are not ashamed of shabby clothes but of lacking knowledge in their belly." As long as you have genuine talent and concrete learning, you can make your way wherever you go. If you always rely on others, "mountains you rely on may collapse; rivers you lean upon may dry up."

"I will never forget a favor I've received, but I will forget all the favors I've done."

Mahayana Buddhism stresses returning kindness and never seeking revenge. When you owe a debt of gratitude, always think, "For each tiny drop of kindness I receive, I will return a gushing river." The mathematician Hua Luogeng said, "I will never forget a favor I've received, but I will forget all the favors I've done." Similarly, if others hold animosity toward you, forget it as soon as possible, and avoid obsessing over it or taking it to heart.

Good-hearted people try never to hold grudges against people who hurt them. An ancient Mahayana Buddhist story illustrates the wisdom of this. One evening, on the way back to his monastery, a monk was caught in a rainstorm, with no sign that it would let up. The monk saw a large house nearby and wondered if he might be allowed to stay there for the night. When the monk rang the bell at the gate, a servant came to answer. After asking what the monk wanted, the servant replied coldly, "My master has no interest in monks. You'd better find someplace else."

The monk then said, "It's raining so hard, and there are no other houses nearby; would you please do me this one favor?"

The servant replied, "I can't make this decision. I will have to ask my master." He went to ask his master and reported back to the monk that the master would not allow him to stay. The monk begged to stay under the eaves for one night, but the servant still shook his head. Having no other option, the monk took his leave, but he first asked for the name of the servant's master. He then rushed back to the monastery in the rain and arrived completely soaked.

Three years later, the wealthy owner of the mansion fell deeply in love with a woman and took her as a concubine. One day, she asked if she could go to the monastery to offer incense and pray for blessings, and the owner went with her. At the monastery, he happened to see his name on a very conspicuous plaque with a prayer for his longevity. He was very surprised and asked a novice monk about it.

The novice said, "Our abbot wrote this three years ago. One night he came home in a rainstorm and told us that he hadn't made a good connection with a benefactor, so he wrote this prayer for him. Since then, he has recited sutras and dedicated merit to him in the hope of disentangling this enmity and with the wish for him to be free from suffering and obtain happiness. If you want more details, then I will have to check . . ." The wealthy man realized what had happened and felt ashamed. He went on to become a devoted benefactor of the monastery, making offerings year round.

This is a story about fixing a bad connection. Would you have done the same? When others refuse to help you or even hurt you, are you still willing to extend goodwill to them or spend three years reciting sutras for them? The point is that in Mahayana Buddhism, we don't take revenge on an enemy; we put our efforts into doing favors instead. As Mark Twain said, "Forgiveness is the fragrance that the violet sheds on the heel that has crushed it."

If You Can't Bear Suffering, It's Your Loss

Some people think that suffering prevents peace and happiness, so they can't accept it. This is a superficial outlook. For those able to transform suffering into motivation, suffering is a tremendous resource. Those who have heard the Buddha's life story know that it was only after witnessing the sufferings of old age, sickness, and death for the first time that the Buddha thought of renouncing worldly life and seeking liberation. It was also because of tremendous suffering that the nun Uppalavanna renounced worldly life, devoted herself to practice, and finally achieved arhatship. There have been hardly any great masters who didn't experience tremendous suffering before achieving great things.

Once, before he became the British prime minister, Winston Churchill attended a gathering of successful businessmen. One businessman told Churchill about his traumatic childhood as an impoverished orphan and said, "Suffering: is it humiliation or treasure? When you overcome suffering, it is your treasure; when suffering overcomes you, it is your humiliation." This short remark deeply touched Churchill. Inspired by this spirit, he became among the most celebrated politicians in British history.

Working through our current hardships gives us the courage to triumph over future ones. For anyone working to become more courageous, suffering can become an ideal source of growth. An indolent life without hardship of any kind is just like an empty ship, easily overturned by a storm.

The Wisdom of Patience

On the journey of life, we can't always have a wide, smooth road, a gentle breeze, and beautiful sunshine. When the going gets tough and anger arises, the wisdom of patience is crucial.

Once, there was a minister called Jin Jian. The emperor gave him five hundred taels (about forty pounds) of gold and told him to buy "the best thing in the world." He traveled to many countries but was unable to fulfill his mission.

One day, he heard an old man call out in the street, "Wisdom for sale! Wisdom for sale! Who wants to buy wisdom?"

The minister thought, "This is something we don't have in our country." He asked the old man the price.

"Five hundred taels of gold, but you have to pay in advance," the old man replied. The minister gave him the gold. The old man spoke clearly, in a mellow and full tone of voice. He said, "This is the genuine wisdom of life, eleven words in total. Be sure to remember it: Before getting mad, ease up. Before taking action, think it through."

Hearing this, the minister felt terrible regret and shame that the gold had been wasted. Cursing the old man, he headed back to his own country.

When he got home, it was already the middle of the night. Walking into the bedroom, he saw that there was someone lying beside his wife. Losing his temper, he thought, "How dare this wench sleep with some-one behind my back!" Enraged, he drew out his sword, ready to thrust it into his wife. Just then, he remembered the old man's eleven words, and he stopped and examined the situation more closely. It was then he saw that the person lying beside his wife was actually his own mother! His wife was ill, and his mother had come to take care of her. The minister then realized that each one of those eleven words was as precious as a jewel. Had he not recalled them, he would have made a tragic blunder. How could five hundred taels of gold compare with the lives of his wife and mother?

Sometimes misfortune occurs due to simple mistakes. Becoming angry about something unreasonable or getting overly emotional might prompt you to do terrible things in a matter of seconds. We must avoid making decisions or acting impetuously when angry. Anger is like a summer storm: it can appear suddenly, but after a short time, the clouds, wind, and rain disappear, and the sky is clear again.

When anger arises in you, try to just pause for a moment, relax, inhale deeply, and give yourself a chance to calm down. You may well avoid doing something stupid!

Don't Be One-Track Minded

In life, some people are flexible: they use different strategies to adapt to different circumstances. Some, on the contrary, are always "one-track minded," treating everything with exactly the same thought, so that many times they go for wool but come home shorn.

Once upon a time, a goldsmith and a carpenter were traveling together. While passing through a wild area, they were stopped by a bandit. Soon the bandit had stripped the carpenter of even his clothes, but the goldsmith managed to make a swift escape, hiding himself in the nearby brush.

The carpenter was a simple man, and he believed that honesty was always the best policy. He had sewn a gold coin in the collar of his jacket, and remembering this, he said to the bandit, "There is a gold coin hidden in my jacket. I'd like to take it back."

The bandit asked, "Where is it?"

The carpenter removed the stitches of the collar and showed the bandit the gold coin. He then said quite earnestly, "This is genuine gold. If you do not believe me, you can ask my friend in the brush over there. He is an excellent goldsmith." The bandit then found the goldsmith and robbed him of his clothes and belongings, too.

This carpenter was not flexible at all. He could not adapt his behavior to the circumstances at hand. Not only did he incur loss for himself, but he also brought trouble for his companion.

In dealing with complicated people or issues, if we are unable to adjust our behavior to the situation, we are unlikely to get a good result. It is like a sharp arrow shot from a powerful bow. It is only an effective weapon if the shooter has good aim. If the arrow hits something hard, such as a rock face, it only breaks itself.

A Short-Tempered Person Drives
Loved Ones Away

We can define anger as an aversion that can vary in intensity. It can range from complaint or criticism, through rage and abuse, up to the intent to kill or destroy.

What is the result for those full of anger and hatred? Their happiness disappears. They are typically in a state of misery, restlessness, and sleeplessness. In a story of one of the Buddha's previous lives it says, "Hatred instantly turns our face ugly. Even if we are bedecked in the most beautiful jewels, no beauty will be seen. Even if we are lying in the most comfortable bed, we can't fall asleep, squirming back and forth as if lying on thorns." People who are angry usually suffer from health problems like hypertension, heart disease, upset stomachs, insomnia, and paranoia. No matter how great their wealth, how high their position, or how many gifts they give to others, if they consistently become angry and hurt others' feelings, the people around them won't appreciate their kindness and will resent them.

There are plenty of historical examples where, by constantly losing their temper, some powerful person or other drives their followers to betray them, which leads to their death. No matter how generous you are, you won't win the trust of others or accomplish your aims if you don't release your mind from hatred and anger.

That said, once anger has arisen in you, you shouldn't suppress it. Instead use different methods to counteract it. As long as anger remains suppressed, it accumulates energy like a volcano, and the greater the suppression, the more energy is accumulated until it finally erupts.

How do you counteract hatred? The answer is wisdom.

Guo Ziyi was one of the wealthiest ministers of China during the Tang dynasty. He was a general who had steadily held his position through four different emperors. During that time of endless war, Guo Ziyi's enemies dug up his ancestral grave. When he heard this news, Guo Ziyi cried out in dismay, but he didn't take revenge or hold a grudge. He said, "So many people have died in all these endless wars, and countless ancestral graves have been desecrated out of hatred. I am, after all, a general leading armies in battle. Many of my own soldiers have also vandalized others' ancestral graves. Now it's my turn to suffer. I too am an unworthy descendant."

Guo Ziyi's first response was to generalize the misdeed of his opponent. Desecrating ancestral graves was a typical consequence of war. His second response was to question his own behavior, thinking, "Hasn't my army also dug up others' ancestral graves?" His third response was to think, "It's my own fault; I shouldn't blame others." When faced with the desecration of his ancestral grave, he was able to contain his animosity, which shows his great patience. Guo Ziyi's fortune wasn't without cause—this is how he attained his success.

When things happen in our lives that make us angry, we can turn to the following four thoughts. First, there are no completely vicious people in this world. The reason that they seem vicious is because they are driven by the winds of karma and afflictive emotions and so should be forgiven.

Second, life is like a dream—it's best not to cling to it too much, for otherwise endless misery will arise.

Third, all sentient beings are in their essential nature buddhas. My anger wasn't triggered by the person but was triggered by their afflictive emotions. If I'm angry, it's equivalent to being angry at afflictive emotions, which is stupid.

Fourth, if the problem can be solved, there's no need to get angry, and if it can't, what use is getting angry?

When anger arises, learn to observe your mind. Often we don't get angry when the event happens. It's only later that anger creeps in, and it continues to proliferate if we fail to rein it in, in time. Sometimes we ourselves add fuel to our anger. The best method when faced with harm or adversity is to use wisdom to tame your mind. Avoid giving in to anger and allowing it to grow fierce. Otherwise, it will become like the single spark that eventually burns down an entire forest of merit.

To Reduce Your Suffering,
Recite the Mantra of Avalokiteshvara

When I was a child, I developed strong faith in Avalokiteshvara, the bodhisattva of compassion. There were different reasons for this: I was born into a Buddhist family, I had unshakable faith in Buddhism from childhood onward, and I was surrounded by this mantra, since it is recited by virtually everyone in Tibet.

When I was a child, our standard of living was far below today's, and our home was quite humble—nothing like today's high-rises—but people had very pure hearts. Growing up in that kind of atmosphere, I recited the mantra of Avalokiteshvara every day while I herded yaks. I can't remember exactly how many times I repeated it, but it was easily several million times.

In my hometown, everybody recites the mantra of Avalokiteshvara. Every family is familiar with it and understands its value. Even if some people aren't so clear about its meaning, they still repeat it every day. The number of accumulated repetitions is incredible. Those of my parents' generation reach a hundred million repetitions or more. This is commonplace in Tibet.

Why is the mantra of Avalokiteshvara so important? In the chapter on listening to the Dharma in the *Wish-Granting Treasury*, the Tibetan master Longchenpa mentions a text called the *Karandavyuha Sutra*, which explains the merit of the mantra and the name of Avalokiteshvara. Longchenpa writes, "The merit of this sutra is immense. It's like a blazing fire that can burn up the negative karma that we have accumulated over beginningless time. It's like clear water that can clean away our karmic obscurations and defilements. It's like a gale wind that can blow away all the obstacles of our body, speech, and mind."

The mantra of Avalokiteshvara is *Om mani padme hum*. Another version adds *hrih* at the end—the seed syllable of Avalokiteshivara—so that it becomes *Om mani padme hum hrih*.

As long as you are sincere and have faith in Avalokiteshvara, there's no need to worry about or standardize the pronunciation. People in China will certainly pronounce the mantra very differently from those in America. Even Tibetan pronunciation varies greatly between Lhasa and eastern Tibet, where I live. As long as you have faith, the merit is no different. Even if the pronunciation is incorrect, merit is still accumulated.

Once, an old monk was out walking when he saw red light radiating from a mountain. He thought that it must be coming from some great practitioner. He decided to climb the mountain and find out, and he came across an old woman. She told him she had recited *Om mani padme nyu* every day for several decades.

The old monk said kindly, "Ah, your pronunciation is incorrect. The correct way to recite is *Om mani padme hum*!" Upon hearing this, the old woman was heartbroken, thinking her practice of several decades was in vain. Feeling dejected, she nonetheless corrected her pronunciation right away.

The old monk left for the foot of the mountain. When he looked back up at the mountain, he saw that the light rays were gone. Realizing what had happened, he immediately went back to the old woman, and told her, "I was joking with you! Your pronunciation of *Om mani padme nyu* was fine!" The old woman beamed and went back to her old pronunciation, and sure enough, the light rays reappeared on the mountain.

So the mantra works if it's recited with sincerity. Even if you don't say it properly, you will certainly experience its blessings. If, however, you recite the mantra insincerely or you are distracted by conceptual thoughts like regret or suspicion, then even if you say every syllable accurately and articulately, you won't have a genuine experience of its blessings.

Five Ways to Dispel Suffering

The great Indian scholar Aryadeva divided human suffering into two types: mental and physical. He wrote, "The privileged suffer in mind and the underprivileged in body. Because of these two kinds of suffering, they feel misery every day in this world." In other words, people in privileged circumstances may be free from many physical hardships but they still experience mental suffering. An example is stress at work, such as worrying about the competition or the sadness of being "lonely at the top." People in underprivileged situations, on the other hand, suffer from lack of food and clothing or from having to do strenuous physical labor. One or both of these kinds of suffering usually torment any living being.

Life is full of suffering, but a lot of people don't recognize this, so a little bit of frustration causes them to blame others and curse their fate, "God! It's not fair! Why am I so unlucky? Why do I never get a break?" They don't understand that this is actually the nature of cyclic existence.

So what can we do when facing suffering? Buddhism has many answers, including the following approaches. Even if some habitual tendencies are so deeply rooted that they can't be immediately and completely cut off, if we persevere, our suffering will diminish sooner or later.

1. Help sentient beings and not yourself.

When you feel miserable, the first thing to do is recognize that the origin of suffering is self-attachment or, in other words, selfishness. In order to eliminate suffering, we have to uproot its cause. One way to do this is to study Buddhist sutras and commentaries so that we can transform selfishness through the selfless spirit of the Mahayana. There are people who used to experience many afflictive emotions, but after studying the Mahayana teachings and devoting themselves to helping sentient beings with activities like charity and volunteer work, their misery disappeared. This method of dispelling suffering by helping others is most effective if you have cultivated loving-kindness, compassion, and bodhichitta, which is the altruistic wish to free all beings from suffering by becoming a buddha yourself. But even if you haven't cultivated these mindstates, you can at least cultivate traditional morality and goodwill.

2. Transform happiness and suffering into the path.

There's another method whereby you can transform suffering into the path. Even though an experience may be painful, if you change your thinking, you can view that experience not as suffering but as a tool.

This method was explained in great detail in Thokmé Sangpo's *Song of Happiness*. For example, this text tells us:

> When I'm ill, I'm happy,
> because karmic obscurations can be eliminated through illness.
> When I'm healthy, I'm still happy,
> because a healthy body can be used to do virtuous deeds.
>
> When I'm rich, I'm happy,
> because I can make offerings to the worthy and give alms to the
>   poor.
> When I'm poor, I'm still happy,
> because it helps me get rid of attachment to money and material
>   goods.

To succeed in life, you have to experience suffering. Genuinely wise people never fear suffering but instead transform every tribulation into a steppingstone to liberation.

Once, a farmer's donkey fell into a dried-up well. Despite considerable fretting, the farmer couldn't think of a way to save it. In the end, he thought, "This donkey is already old, and it's also time to fill in this well. It's no use wasting energy on saving the donkey." He asked all his neighbors to help him fill in the well with earth.

The donkey quickly realized what was happening and moaned in panic, but after a while, it calmed down. The farmer couldn't help looking down into the well and was amazed by what he saw: the donkey quickly shook off every shovel full of soil that came down and then stamped it firmly under its feet. In no time at all, the donkey reached the opening of the well, jumped out, and ran away.

Our life is similar in that misery keeps raining down on us. But no matter how much misery strikes you, just shake it off like dust and soil, stamp it firmly under your feet, and never let it bury you. Like that, you too will be able to escape the suffering of the ocean of cyclic existence, just like the donkey that escaped from the well.

3. Practice the exchange of self and others: giving and taking.

Another helpful way to dispel suffering is called the exchange of self and others. For instance, if you're very sick in bed, your reputation is tarnished, or you become penniless, you can make this aspiration: "There are so many people in this world as miserable as I am. May their suffering ripen on me and let me experience it for them. May they be free from suffering and obtain happiness." Then, with each exhalation, visualize all your peace and happiness turning into white smoke and going to all sentient beings. With each inhalation, visualize all their suffering turning into black smoke and entering into you. This is the best way to dispel suffering. If we can practice this every time we encounter misery, then the suffering we have to experience becomes worthwhile. With time and practice, our egocentrism will gradually decrease.

4. Cultivate mental strength.

Having mental strength means being able to endure adversity. With this quality you won't easily surrender in the face of suffering. I have read some biographies of influential people and found that the reason they were so successful was because they were strong-minded. Even when facing incredible adversity, they bravely solved those difficulties and never gave up. In contrast, some people fail because their minds are so fragile that they can't bear even mild blows—a small frustration makes them sink into despair.

So what is the key to success or failure? The Song dynasty statesman and writer Su Dongpo said, "The great figures in history didn't just have talent beyond that of ordinary people; they also possessed a dauntless and persistent will."

5. Mipham Rinpoche's method for improving your mood

There is a practice in Tibetan Buddhism to dispel suffering and lift our spirits that is very straightforward. First, gaze straight into the space in front of you, relax naturally without any clinging, expand your mind as widely as possible, and then rest calmly in this state. Next, chant *Tayata om tsomo milena deka tamo svaha* seven or 108 times. This practice can improve your mood and relationships and pacify afflictions.

You don't have to use all of the methods described above. Since everyone has different preferences, choose a method that suits you best. As with certain ailments, some people prefer herbs or acupuncture, some like getting massages, and some get shots from their doctors. No matter what method you use, the purpose is the same—to ease suffering.

Finding Happiness through Mantra Recitation

Anyone who has visited Tibet notices a common thread uniting the people: young or old, man or woman, monk, nun, or householder, everyone has a *mala*—a Tibetan rosary—moving from bead to bead in their hands. This mala is neither jewelry nor an amulet to dispel disaster or demons. Rather, it's an essential tool for counting mantra recitations. Many Tibetans recite these mantras diligently for their entire lives, accumulating totals in the hundreds of millions.

Ultimately, the mantras of buddhas and bodhisattvas are indivisible from the buddhas and bodhisattvas themselves. The mantra of Avalokiteshvara is the bodhisattva Avalokiteshvara himself, and the mantra of Manjushri, the bodhisattva of wisdom, is Manjushri himself.

When we recite these mantras, we are able to have a complete meeting of minds with these buddhas and bodhisattvas. The renowned master Mipham Rinpoche said in his *Luminous Essence,* "On the ultimate level, all phenomena are undivided within the expanse of purity and equality, the great body of truth. On the relative level, there's no difference between the form of the deity and its mantra, insofar as both are merely manifestations of wisdom that arise for the welfare of those needing guidance."

Your mind's encounter with buddhas and bodhisattvas awakens different aspects of your potential. In the past, each of the buddhas and bodhisattvas aspired to benefit beings through a specific quality or virtue. When we recite their mantras, we cultivate the particular quality or blessing associated with that buddha or bodhisattva.

For instance, the bodhisattva Manjushri is the deity associated with the wisdom aspect of all the buddhas of the three times. By reciting the mantra of Manjushri, we activate our wisdom. Avalokiteshvara is the deity associated with the compassionate aspect of all the buddhas of the three times, so by reciting the mantra of Avalokiteshvara, we enhance our compassion. Through reciting mantras, not only can the transcendent merit of liberation be perfected but also worldly benefits can be accomplished, such as having a long life and enjoying good health.

Some people won't accept this and say, "That's ridiculous! How is that possible?" In fact the viability and potency of mantras can be established in different ways—through personal experience, scriptural authority, and logical reasoning.

Unfortunately, nowadays many people believe that whatever can't be proven by science, such as the blessings of mantras, the existence of past and future lives, karma, and so forth, must be untrue. Technically, though, just because science can't prove something does not mean it is refuted. To blindly believe everything that has the veneer of science is ridiculous as well. It makes better sense to take a rational attitude toward things we don't know, neither too readily accepting nor too quick to dismiss. A true scientist is open-minded and recognizes there is much we can neither prove nor disprove at this time. Science still has a lot to learn about the mind in particular.

There are people with some familiarity with Buddhism, especially in China, who say that it's better to avoid the tantric practices because there are too many mantras, which they think are not an authentic part of Buddhism. This view is also narrow-minded. Even the sutras contain many mantras, such as the mantras in the *Shurangama Sutra*, the dharani for rebirth in the Pure Land of Great Bliss, the great compassion mantra, the ten short mantras that are part of morning and evening practices for daily chanting, and so forth. The *Golden Light Sutra* says, "Even bodhisattvas at the highest level need the protection of mantras, let alone ordinary people!" Even at the end of the widely chanted *Heart Sutra* there's a mantra, about which it says that it is "the unsurpassed mantra, the mantra equal to the unequaled." If, as some people in China believe, mantras are akin to catastrophes or devils, then how are we to explain these examples?

That said, as I mentioned before, we shouldn't blindly accept or deny anything, even if it is said to come from the Buddha himself. It is important to examine whether something is correct or not. Even the Buddha and Buddhist masters encourage this, providing us with the analytical tools of Middle Way philosophy and of logic and epistemology. I have no doubt that the Buddha wants us to see the true nature of all phenomena for ourselves rather than relying on blind faith!

Mantras for Averting Suffering and Obtaining Happiness

Buddha Shakyamuni

If you wish to alleviate the stress of life and work, one of the simplest and most practical types of meditation is to gaze at an image of Buddha Shakyamuni with full absorption for a while, then close your eyes and bring the image to mind. When the mental image starts to blur, open your eyes and gaze at the image again for a while, and then close your eyes and visualize it again. Keep practicing like this until the image appears clearly in your mind. If you wish to develop concentration, this method brings the greatest blessings.

You can also recite the mantra of Buddha Shakyamuni, which is excellent for subduing your mental afflictions: *Tadyatha om muni muni mahamuniye svaha*.

Amitayus

If you wish to lengthen your life or someone else's, or to avoid an early grave or unexpected death, pray wholeheartedly to Amitayus, the buddha of long life. To do this, mindfully recite his mantra: *Om amarani jivantiye svaha*.

Vajrasattva

When regret arises for all the negative deeds you have committed in the past, whether intentionally or unintentionally, recite the mantra of Vajrasattva: *Om vajrasattva hum*. At the same time, visualize nectar descending from Vajrasattva and rinsing away all your negative karma. This practice gradually eliminates all kinds of negative karma.

The Medicine Buddha

Praying to the Medicine Buddha with absorption and faith by reciting *Om bhaishajye bhaishajye mahabhaishajye raja samudgate svaha* can increase longevity, dispel all sorts of diseases and disasters, and as a bonus, make you appear more dignified.

Amitabha

At the time of death, if you can recite *Namo Amitabha* wholeheartedly while visualizing the sublime body of the Buddha Amitabha, you can become free from the suffering and fear of death and feel peaceful, happy, and physically at ease. Those who are fortunate can even take rebirth in the Pure Land of Great Bliss after death. It's even better if the dying person recites it together with other people.

Padmasambhava

If you pray devoutly to Padmasambhava and with concentration recite his mantra, *Om ah hum vajra guru padma siddhi hum*, you can avert negative events like conflicts, diseases, and sudden misfortune. Obstacles to practice will be eliminated, and wishes will be swiftly fulfilled.

Tara

If you pray devoutly to Tara, and with concentration recite her mantra, *Om tare tuttare ture svaha*, evil curses, suicidal ideations, and diseases can be annihilated; afflictive emotions can be pacified; fears can be dispelled; and wealth, influence, and fame can be obtained. In the present era, this practice brings results most swiftly.

Kshitigarbha

In order to fulfill your wishes, enhance the roots of virtue, increase merit and wealth, or transfer the consciousness of the deceased to a favorable rebirth, you can recite *Namo bodhisattva kshitigarbha* and pray for his blessings.

Manjushri

If you would like to activate your inner wisdom and distinguish what should be adopted from what should be abandoned, recite the mantra of Manjushri, *Om arapachana dhih*. In particular, for those who are still in school, reciting the mantra of Manjushri can help improve academic performance.

Avalokiteshvara

If you're in a dangerous situation or disaster and you single-mindedly recite *Om mani padme hum*, it can transform difficult situations into favorable ones and misfortune into good fortune.

Garudas

In order to benefit sentient beings, buddhas and bodhisattvas manifest in the form of the eagle-like garudas, who embody the mind's pure essence. If you wholeheartedly pray to the garudas, you can obtain strength, ward off negative influences, and experience relief from ailments like seizures.

These are just some examples of the benefits of deity practices. In fact, each mantra or name bestows boundless merit. However, in order to help you choose which mantra or name to recite, I have described their main benefits so that you can choose the one that's best suited to your needs.

While reciting the mantras or names of buddhas or bodhisattvas, it's very important to gaze at or visualize their physical form. This helps us to concentrate on the object without becoming distracted and to become open to their blessings. In fact, just looking at an image of a buddha accumulates merit and wards off obstacles. The *Avatamsaka Sutra* says, "If someone catches sight of a buddha, he or she will be free from all obstacles, accumulate infinite merit, and gain accomplishment on the path to enlightenment." Even if you look at the Buddha's image with hatred or defiance, you still have established a connection with the Buddha and will benefit from it in future lives.

If we place a statue of the Buddha in a high, clean place and sincerely perform prostrations, make offerings, and pray to it regularly, and if we practice according to the Buddhist teachings, as time goes on we'll receive many intangible blessings. We'll gradually experience fewer afflictive emotions, less stress, and less suffering.

I'm certain that no matter what you wish for, as long as you pray wholeheartedly to the Buddha, you're bound to receive help that matches your capacity, your karma, and your circumstances. Even just chanting "Namo Buddha" ("praise to the Buddha") one time could be significant for your present and future lives.

2

Being Like the Buddha

If you habitually seek out others' shortcomings,
you will see in them no saving grace
even if they are bodhisattvas.
The wise adopt a pure perception of everyone.

Keeping Secrets

Don't just try to keep your own secrets—keep others' secrets as well. Some people share everything that's on their minds, particularly when drunk. As the saying goes, "Once a secret is shared, it goes on world tour!" Failing to keep secrets will only disappoint people who trust you.

Once, a woman applied for a position at a multinational company. After the first round of interviews, some of the applicants were asked to take a written test. The woman answered the questions quickly and had no difficulty until she reached the last one. That question was: "Please write down any secrets you know from your last company." She looked around and saw some people answering the question in detail. She thought for a moment and went up to the examiner with the paper in her hand and said, "I'm sorry, but I don't think I can answer this last question. I have an obligation to my former employer." She gave the examiner what she had written up to that point and left.

The next day, she got a letter from the company offering her the job. At the end of the letter, her new boss had written, "People with good professional ethics are exactly what we're looking for." Those who respect others will eventually gain respect, and those who keep others' secrets will win their trust.

Moreover, some things aren't really secrets but are better left unsaid for the benefit of ourselves and others. First, we should keep quiet about our own good qualities. Even if we have a lot of good qualities, we shouldn't brag about them! In most cases, talking about our own merits is regarded as arrogant and will cause others to think all kinds of negative things about us.

Second, we should keep others' faults to ourself. Sometimes we feel annoyed by others' behavior. This annoyance is in fact a sign that our own Buddhist practice is inadequate. When others talk about our faults, either face to face or behind our back, we feel upset. If we put ourselves in other people's shoes, we will quickly lose our penchant for talking about their faults.

Third, we should keep our personal plans secret. It's easy to bring about negative results if we openly advertise our future plans. Everything can change, so it's better not to publicize a plan before its success is assured.

These teachings reflect the advice of highly accomplished masters. The words are simple, but the meaning is profound. I hope you will keep them in mind!

Imagine What Others Might Feel

If you're concerned about how your actions might impact someone, put yourself in their place and ask yourself, "Would I like it if someone did this to me?"

Zi Gong once asked Confucius, "Is there a practice I can use in every aspect of my life?"

Confucius responded with a single word—*forgiveness*—and then said to him, "Never inflict on others anything you don't like for yourself." This is also the golden rule that Jesus taught: "In all things, do to others as you would have them do to you."

Putting yourself in the place of others is also emphasized in Buddhism. For example, the *Way of the Bodhisattva* says:

> What is the difference between oneself and others if both loathe
>   suffering?
> Why does one only protect oneself?
> Therefore, if you're unwilling to accept suffering, never impose it
>   on others,
> because others are unwilling to accept it as well.

There's also a well-known Buddhist story about Hariti, a demoness who had a thousand sons. The youngest was her favorite. She was fond of eating the flesh of little children and continually abducted them and ate them alive. Seeking to put an end to this, the people asked the Buddha for help.

The Buddha used his miraculous powers to catch her youngest son and hide him in his begging bowl. When Hariti arrived home and found her youngest son was missing, she became so upset that she couldn't eat, drink, or sleep. She looked for him for seven days. Finally hearing that the Buddha was omniscient, she went to him for help.

The Buddha said, "You have one thousand sons, and now you're sad about losing just one. Other people have only one or two children, and yet you eat them! Do you think they suffer any less than you do? Don't they suffer that much more?"

Hariti was shocked into understanding and repented, saying, "If my youngest son comes back to me, I will never eat another child again." The Buddha released her youngest son from the begging bowl and returned him to her.

In short, every sentient being wants happiness and avoids suffering. When interacting with others, try putting yourself in their place, especially if you don't see eye to eye.

Returning Favors

Deciding whether someone will be a good friend doesn't have to be difficult. If they appreciate the kindness of others and return that kindness, they will be a good friend. Wise people remember others' kindness and feel disappointed when they don't get a chance to return it. However, people with difficult personalities often don't recognize the things that people do for them. It never occurs to them to return the favor. They think they are entitled to this treatment and may even return kindness with animosity and slander, which reveals just how negative their minds have become.

Once upon a time, there was a father who had wisdom and had earnestly studied the Buddhist teachings. Before he died, he gave his son this final piece of advice, "Serve wise sovereigns and not foolish ones; marry a thoughtful wife and not a selfish one; make friends with the virtuous and avoid the vicious."

This son was so young and impetuous that he wanted to test the truth of his father's advice. He decided to deliberately serve a foolish king and marry a selfish wife, but he made friends with a virtuous person.

One day, he traveled into the mountains with the king. There they camped together in a cave for the night. In the middle of the night, a fierce tiger came into the cave and was about to eat the king. At the last moment, the son leapt in and killed the tiger with his sword, saving the poor king.

Afterward, he said to the king, "I saved your life today. One day you should repay me." Snatched from the jaws of death, the king was overjoyed and agreed.

As time passed, though, the king forgot his promise and showed no sign that he would repay his heroic servant. The son became so annoyed that he stole the king's favorite peacock, and he and his wife ate it. Later, he confessed everything to his virtuous friend.

The king, distraught at his loss, proclaimed that if his peacock were found, the reward would be half the kingdom. The son's friend, noble and kind, didn't expose him. His wife, however, told the king everything.

Captured and about to be sentenced to death, the son said to the king, "It's true that I killed the peacock, but as I once saved your life, you must pardon me!"

The king sneered, "I have so many servants; how can I return every single kindness? You killed my peacock and so you must die!"

Luckily, the good friend had gone to the mountains and caught a peacock that was almost identical to the king's. Arriving just in time, he offered it to the king, exclaiming, "Your majesty, please calm your anger. Here is your peacock!" Having regained "his" peacock, the king forgot all about executing the son.

After this incident, the son decided to test his father's advice in the opposite way. He entered into the service of a wise king and married a thoughtful wife, but he made friends with a depraved person.

One day, while horseback riding in the countryside with the king, something startled the king's horse and it bolted, running hither and thither until they were utterly lost. After many hours, they both became unbearably hungry and thirsty. All the son had to eat was two gooseberries, but he gave one to the king. Gratefully, the king promised, "I will return this kindness." A little while later, they rediscovered their path home and returned to the palace.

To test this king, the son abducted the king's beloved son. Taking the prince's clothes, he gave them to his wicked friend and said, "I've killed the prince." Then he gave the prince to his wife to look after. Grieving the loss of his favorite child, the king announced throughout the kingdom that there would be a large reward for any information about his whereabouts.

Hearing of the reward, the vicious friend immediately betrayed the son. The king wasn't quite convinced by the friend's accusation, and so he summoned the son to confirm his tale. The son immediately admitted to killing the prince, but then he asked the king for forgiveness. The king lamented, "My poor son had such a short life. Even if I kill you, it won't accomplish anything. I forgive you and thus return the kindness you once did me."

Convinced that the king was indeed a wise sovereign who appreciated and repaid others' kindness, the son told the king everything and asked his wife to bring the prince home. As you can imagine, after these experiences, he was utterly convinced of the truth of his father's advice.

Of course, we can't insist that another person appreciate and return kindness while not doing the same ourselves. No matter how small the favor, we should return it as soon as possible and remember what that person did for us. Even if we can't return the favor right away, we can at least appreciate and recollect it.

Faults

As the saying goes, "To err is human." It's impossible to find a person without faults in this world. If you're annoyed by someone's flaws, don't talk about it, and also avoid spreading gossip about someone's private life.

In Jin Ying's *Anthology of Proverbs*, Master Hongyi says, "When sitting quietly, always think about your own faults. When chatting, avoid talking about the faults of others."

He also says, "I don't have enough time to review my own faults every day, so how can there be time for me to criticize the faults of others?"

Some people, however, are very keen on discussing others' faults. As soon as they hear a bit of gossip about someone, they embellish it and gleefully spread the word. Likewise, when angry with someone, they berate them, listing their faults and leaving them in misery. This is destructive behavior. Ancient sages say, "Don't address others' flaws when scolding them." If you want to be virtuous, then no matter what the circumstances, watch your tongue carefully.

Once, there was a wealthy woman who had a wise servant. One day the woman said to her servant, "Go to the market and buy me the best thing you can find." The servant went to the market and returned with a tongue. The woman then said to him, "Go to the market again and buy me the *worst* thing you can find." The servant went back to the market and came back with another tongue.

The woman asked him why he bought tongues both times, and the servant replied, "The tongue is the origin of virtue and nonvirtue. When it behaves well, there's nothing better, and when it behaves badly, there's nothing worse."

What determines whether speech is virtuous is the mind. What we think determines what we say. In order to control our tongue, we must first cultivate inner virtue. When our mind is disciplined, our speech will be as well.

Therefore those with virtue will shut their mouths after hearing about others' bad behavior, keeping their comments to themselves. As the character Vidura says in the *Mahabharata*, "The best virtue is a subdued tongue."

Considering Others

If you put yourself first, others will resent you. It's impossible to be a buddha before you become a good person. Of course, the definition of "good person" may differ for each individual. Some people think a mild temperament and industriousness make a person virtuous. Some think being softhearted makes someone good. Others believe that those with a strong and forthright personality are good people. My own teacher, however, didn't think like this. He said that to become a good person, one should follow these instructions:

Be in accord with others.

This means that you should respect your superiors, seek harmony with your peers, and look after those under you. Basically, try to get along with people as best you can. Avoid glaring at others or stirring up conflict in whatever group you're with.

This doesn't mean we shouldn't have our own opinions and principles. It doesn't mean we should be servile when others are angry with us. It doesn't mean to blindly cater to others' wishes. Rather, it means behaving in accordance with the Dharma, with a disciplined mind. Disagreement and conflict are inevitable. With good ethics and mindfulness, however, we can get along with almost anyone.

There's a metaphor in Tibet, "When a hundred yaks go uphill, *gaba* (a lesser breed of yak) insist on running downhill." People with bad personalities cause trouble everywhere. When taking the bus, for example, they fight with people on the way, and when they get off, everyone is so relieved and feels like cheering.

Of course, it isn't easy to assess someone's personality based on first impressions. Some people might act with tremendous kindness at first, but after a while, they may begin to disappoint. Others might seem difficult at first, but later they begin to impress you and win your trust. It's said, "On a long journey the strength of a horse is discovered; after long association a person's heart is revealed."

Virtue in speech and action

If you're ever in an argument with somebody, objective facts are the most important criteria. Some people blurt out whatever annoys them or whatever pops up into their mind, believing that this is good speech because it is honest. Actually they are just voicing their thoughts. Genuine virtuous speech means resolving conflict with your conscience as witness. Avoid bias toward yourself or others and argue for the side supported by the facts, regardless of the position or wealth of the parties concerned.

The legendary judge Bao Gong, who sentenced an emperor's son-in-law to death, is a well-known example in China. In order to promote righteousness, Bao Gong risked angering the emperor and losing his position rather than ignoring justice and jeopardizing the public's confidence in their government. If we can learn to be more like this, even if others misunderstand us, harm us, or slander us, we will have a clear conscience.

Right motivation

If you live in accord with others but have negative motives, there's no chance for you to become a good person. Some people speak clearly and logically but secretly harbor malice. The result is that whatever they do is in vain, because the mind is the root of everything. As the Tibetan master Tsongkhapa said, a kind heart creates a virtuous path; malice leads to the path of wickedness.

These principles are essential. My teacher added one more thing: "If you want to benefit yourself, the best strategy is to benefit others first." For ordinary people, it's impossible to completely ignore the self, but in the process of considering yourself, be aware that if it causes harm to others, you won't get what you want.

Once, I was on an airplane sitting next to a young man who seemed very intelligent. It turned out that he was the general manager of a company. He made it clear that he didn't believe in Buddhism, but in our conversation there were points that we agreed on. For example, he said, "We should be good people and help others. In fact, in order to run a successful enterprise, we have to help people around us—this is the only way that we can survive. People are intelligent. If I blindly consider my own interests, they will see what's going on, and I will end up achieving nothing." What he said was perfectly reasonable. No matter what you do, if you always consider yourself first, others will resent you, but if you help others as best you can, they will respect you.

My teacher also said, "Through my experience over the years, I have found that many people have no idea how to be a good person. They are selfishly concerned with themselves every day. Sadly, acting in this way, their wishes won't be realized.

"For instance, sometimes when young people fall in love, they try to control the other person and are very possessive, but the outcome is the opposite of what they want. Others, however, put their heart and soul into supporting and helping the person they love to flourish, and eventually they win a place in that person's affections."

What a pity how few people understand this.

Ignoring Flattery

Some people are highly skilled at flattering and complimenting others. In particular, people in positions of power often have obsequious aides who cater to all their likes and dislikes, singing their praises. Such flattery may be appealing to vain or insecure people, but those who are wise feel uncomfortable with such treatment.

Back in the eighties, a young woman who had just graduated from college was on a train home while waiting to find a job. She was eager to go home again but was also wondering about her future. At one station, a woman in plain clothes holding a baby got on and sat in the empty seat beside her. After exchanging glances, the woman started a conversation.

"Young lady, you look like you were born into a very well-educated family. You must be a scholar or a doctor."

"No, I just got my bachelor's degree."

"In any case, I envy you. Actually, I wanted to go to college when I was younger, but my family was so poor that I could only go to school for a couple of days. I can't even write my own name. It makes me sad. Later I started a small business and made some money. Friends advised me to start another company, but I'm afraid I'll be tricked, because I have no real business knowledge. Right now I'm going to the city to sign a contract. Could you please help me? I will pay all your expenses. If you'd like to run the business with me, I'm willing to collaborate. I have money, and clearly you are very intelligent and bound for success."

Feeling flattered, the college graduate agreed. The woman invited her to get off the train with her and made a phone call. She said, "You must be tired, let's rest at my aunt's house." They took a bus and arrived at a village in the suburbs. Walking into a high-walled courtyard, they were led to the house by the master, a middle-aged man. After a short conversation, he gave the woman a pack of something. Then the woman told the young woman, "Please make yourself at home. My cousin said that my aunt is feeling sick, and I want to go see her. You rest here, and I'll be back in a minute."

So the young woman waited, but the woman never returned. In fact, the woman was luring and selling people. She had sold the girl to that middle-aged man as his wife. Later, the college graduate managed to escape and told everyone about her traumatic experience.

Nowadays some people aren't careful when making friends. They are lured in by smooth words and empty promises. Later they lament, "I was so naive! I didn't know!" Don't let flattery blind you and impair your judgment.

Dealing with Irrational People

Mixing with rude or irrational people invites frustration. If you get into a disagreement with such people, if you make one remark, they will give you ten in return. Some people might say, "Irrational people are unavoidable!" This may be true, but you can still treat them with patience by keeping silent or just saying what they want to hear for the time being.

Once, two bad-tempered people argued the whole day over some trivial issue. By dusk they still hadn't come to an agreement, so they parted ways. That night, one of them went to see a local elder and told him what had happened. He asked the elder to give his opinion on the matter, and the elder said, "You're absolutely right." The man was satisfied and went home.

Later the other man visited the same elder and asserted how reasonable his position was. After hearing him out, the elder smiled and said to him, "You're obviously correct." That man also left feeling happy.

Seeing this, the elder's attendant was totally confused and asked, "Why did you agree with both of them? If both are correct, why did they argue?"

The elder said, "The subject they were debating was meaningless. If they continue to argue, it will only make them unhappy. There's no need to use reason with people like that. I just agreed so that they would feel satisfied." This did in fact end their dispute.

Some people argue meaninglessly just to gain the upper hand, while the wise just shake their heads, as though watching children fight over toys.

The Impact of Negative Influences

Negative people are harmful to your life and your Buddhist practice. Cultivating good qualities is difficult, and it's easy to fall into vice. Even wise people can engage in unethical activity if they don't exercise caution in choosing whom they associate with. Gungthangpa's *Similes of Trees and Water* says,

> Even a majestic tree
> is felled if its roots are flooded.
> Even virtuous people with good qualities
> are pulled down by false friends.

The *Thirty-Seven Practices of a Bodhisattva* by Thokmé Sangpo says, "When a friendship with someone increases the three poisons, dampens the activities of listening, reflecting, and meditating, and destroys loving-kindness and compassion, then giving up such a friendship is the practice of a bodhisattva." In other words, if we find a friendship is increasing our afflictions and taking us away from the path of love and compassion, we should consider leaving that friendship behind. We need to choose our friends wisely.

In Liu Yiqing's *New Account of the Tales of the World*, there is a story about two friends named Guan Ning and Hua Xin. They ate at the same table, studied in the same room, and slept in the same bed, each like the other's shadow. Once, when they were weeding a crop, Guan Ning hit a gold ingot. He ignored it and continued to weed. When Hua Xin saw this, he dropped his hoe and rushed over to pick up the gold.

Guan Ning kept working but scolded him: "Wealth should be gained through your own efforts. A moral person shouldn't covet property gained without work." Hearing this, Hua Xin stopped and went back to work, but he was frustrated about leaving the gold. Guan Ning noticed this but didn't say anything more; he just discreetly shook his head.

Another time they were reading together, as they often did, sitting on the same mat, when they heard a commotion. A high official was passing by with a troop of people playing on gongs and drums and a crowd gathering around them. It was a distracting scene. Guan Ning turned a deaf ear to the clamor as if nothing were happening. Hua Xin, however, was captivated. He complained that he couldn't see the procession from there, stopped reading, and ran into the street to join the revelry.

Guan Ning was very disappointed. When Hua Xin returned, he cut the mat into two pieces and said sadly, "Our ambitions and inclinations are too different. From now on, we'll be separate like this mat."

If you associate with undisciplined people, watching them lose their integrity out of self-interest again and again, your own wrong views may be reinforced, and your Buddhist practice will suffer.

The Benefits of Pure Perception

For us ordinary people, the appearances projected by the mind are mostly impure. As great masters have said, "Buddhas see every sentient being as a buddha, demons see all sentient beings as demons, and ordinary people see all sentient beings as ordinary." Just because someone appears offensive to us, we should be slow to judge, since we cannot be sure what distortions cloud our view.

Some people become irritated easily by others and are very "talented" at diagnosing others' faults. They can see a louse on the face of others but cannot see even a yak on their own face. They cannot see their own faults even when they are as huge and obvious as Mount Meru.

The *Treasury of Aphorisms* says, "The noble ones examine their own faults, while the inferior only look at others' faults." Virtuous people maintain an inward awareness every moment, so that they can perfect their virtue. However, people with unruly minds place their eyes externally, searching for others' flaws without missing even a trace. They scrutinize others, not letting even a hint of a fault pass. Sometimes they even wear magnifiers, attempting to find bones in an egg. They are blind to others' merits, but once they come upon a fault, they act like they have found a precious jewel.

As you may know, the realization of a person cannot be judged from external appearances. In the past, the eighty-four great Indian adepts did not outwardly behave in accord with the Dharma. Some of them were butchers, some prostitutes, and others performed the menial jobs of the lower castes. However, their wisdom and merit far surpassed ordinary people. They appeared ordinary, but they were great bodhisattvas within. It is said that to speak ill of the enlightened one incurs terrible negative karma. Since people are not always what they appear, we should not rush to judgment. A pile of ashes might appear harmless, but if there are still sparks within it, you may still get burned.

It is better to enjoy hearing your own faults than to enjoy hearing the faults of others. If you become aware of your own shortcomings, you can fix them. But if you habitually look for others' shortcomings, you see no saving grace in them even if they are real buddhas or bodhisattvas. The wise adopt a pure perception of everyone.

Working with Criticism

When someone offers criticism that is constructive, it's good practice to accept it and try to see the person as a friend or teacher. When others point out your faults, if you don't become angry but instead are genuinely willing to work on improving yourself, you will avoid alienating those who can help you most. On the contrary, if you're unwilling to hear criticism and reflect on your mistakes, flying into a defensive rage, beneficial friends will eventually give up and avoid you.

When Confucius first assisted the king of the state of Lu, it took only three months for the state to become orderly and peaceful. It was said that it was so peaceful that nobody snatched up others' lost things on the road, and people slept at night with their doors unlocked. All the weapons were stored away, and the horses were set free in the mountains. Great peace pervaded the whole state. The king of the neighboring state of Qi was jealous of the results of Confucius's management. To undermine Lu's increasing strength, Qi's ministers started looking for ways to upset Lu's government.

What idea did Qi come up with? They sent a group of beautiful women skilled at singing and dancing to the court of the king of Lu. The plan was to intoxicate the king with sensory pleasure so that he would not have the energy to manage the country. Just as hoped, the king of Lu spent all day and night dancing, singing, and drinking with the beguiling women. He disregarded everything else, not even showing up at his court for three consecutive days.

Confucius sternly reprimanded the king and exhorted him not to be so indulgent. The king, however, rejected his advice. Blind to his own faults, he told Confucius to mind his own business. Confucius decided that Lu was a lost cause, and so he resigned, and the kingdom of Lu fell back into strife.

Even successful and disciplined people can sometimes fail to notice their own remaining faults, so reminders from others are vital. If you get angry when your faults are pointed out and are only happy to hear compliments, there's no way for you to correct your mistakes, and your words and actions will gradually deteriorate. If this happens, harmful companions will gradually come closer to you, and helpful ones will slowly fall away.

Steadfast Friends

Sometimes it can be hard to distinguish helpful companions from harmful ones. It's especially difficult to know whether a friendship is genuine when everything is going well. It's in adversity that genuine affection is revealed.

One of Aesop's fables illustrates this: Two friends were walking down a path when they encountered a bear. There was one small tree nearby, and the first friend jumped and climbed up it without a second thought. His companion had no choice but to lie down, hold his breath, and play dead. The bear approached the one on the ground and sniffed at him. It is said that bears don't eat dead people, and so it left. Afterward, the one in the tree came down and jokingly asked his companion, "What did the bear tell you?"

"The bear gave me a piece of advice," he answered. "Never travel with friends who abandon you at the sign of danger!" Sometimes we only find out who our friends are in a crisis.

I heard a story about an influential government official. A lot of people would come to see him at his house. A neighbor asked him, "Your house is always full of people, but how many friends do you really have?"

He answered, "Come back and ask me when I no longer have this position."

A lot of people have had this experience. When you're successful in life, many people are deferential to you and seek your company. Once you stumble or become ill, however, only a few friends may actually be willing to help you.

Often our most reliable friends are our oldest friends. As the old saying goes, "As age improves the flavor of wine, time enhances friendship." Old friends, those who have been close for many years, always maintain a deep affection for each other. So while we should be wary about associating with nonvirtuous friends, we should also value old friends and not abandon them capriciously.

The genuine value of friendship is to correct and encourage each other to go in a better direction. Old friends know us best and can be a big help. In trivial matters do not haggle with them over every ounce or make a storm in a teacup. It was always said by the ancients, "Remember and do not abandon the old." It teaches us to remember and value old things. In history some famous emperors, such as Liu Xiu, Emperor Guang Wu of the Han dynasty, and Zhu Yuanzang, founder of the Ming dynasty, never gave up old friendships even after they were granted the "mandate of heaven."

For instance, after Zhu Yuanzang became the emperor, he asked his subjects to look throughout the kingdom for his old friend Tian Xing, who had farmed with him when he was young. He wrote a letter himself to his old friend, "Emperor is emperor, Zhu Yuanzang is Zhu Yuanzang. Don't think that I will abandon old friends now that I am the emperor."

Some people, however, once they make it big, become fickle. For them, new friends become extra attractive while old friends become uninteresting. They treat others with a lack of affection and only want friends they "click" with, and so they end up surrounded by people with ulterior motives up their sleeves. Old friends should not be easily abandoned, and new friends should not be too quickly trusted. Relationships that put down roots over time are best able to withstand trials.

Don't Be Ashamed of Not Knowing

The Confucian philosopher Han Yu said, "People aren't born to know everything." There are many things we don't know, and we should never feel ashamed about this. Wise people are modest, curious, and ready to be students. Fools are ashamed to ask others, thinking it will only expose their ignorance. In reality, they need not feel ashamed.

Confucius said, "To know is to know, to not know is to not know, and this is something to know." If you really know something, then you can speak about it, but if you don't know it, simply admit it.

Ding Zhaozhong, winner of the Nobel Prize in Physics, was once asked three questions during a lecture. Each time he answered "I don't know." The questions were:

"Do you believe human beings can find dark matter and antimatter in space?"

"I don't know."

"Can you think of any economic value for the scientific experiments you have done?"

"I don't know."

"Could you talk about the future direction of physics in the next twenty years?"

"I don't know."

At first everyone was surprised by his responses, but a few moments later they broke out in applause. Ding Zhaozhong didn't have to say "I don't know"—he was perfectly capable of giving the audience a credible-sounding answer—but he chose to answer the questions honestly. By saying "I don't know," he revealed his integrity as a scientist.

Concealing a Mistake
Is Worse than Making One

Unintentional errors are mistakes; deliberate wrongdoing is immoral. Sometimes people are careless or poorly trained, and the result of what they do isn't perfect, but since they didn't intend to harm anyone, they were mistaken rather than immoral.

It is the wisdom of the elders that "There's no greater virtue than making up for your mistakes." Everybody makes mistakes, but not everyone owns up to them. Confucius once praised Yan Hui's virtue of not repeating errors. When Yan Hui made a mistake, he would reflect on it, make amends, and never let it happen again.

A student of mine once made a mistake but was inspired by Yan Hui's example and came to me to confess it. He said, "Please give me another chance! If I do it again, I'll eat my hat!"

However, he did it again not very long after. When I asked, "Do you remember what you said?" he dropped his head and said, "Can I have another chance?"

Of course it's not good to repeat a mistake, but it's even worse to conceal one. Many people try to cover up their mistakes, but ethical people try to be open and upright. When they make a mistake, they own it and do their best to change. A Buddhist sutra says that nonvirtue has one good quality: it can be purified.

3

The Certainty of Loss

So many things we feel we cannot put down.
Yet when we do put them down,
we begin to experience real happiness.

Impermanence

Whatever comes together will fall apart. This is the law of impermanence. People we see every day are brought to us by temporary causes and conditions; at some point, we are bound to go our separate ways. As ancient Chinese philosophers say, "No matter how profound the kindness of our parents, we will eventually separate. No matter how devoted a couple is to each other, they will eventually part. Our lives are just like birds sleeping in the same tree who then fly away in different directions at the sound of danger."

I once read a book that related a story of the second president of IBM, Thomas J. Watson Jr. He had been suffering from serious heart disease, and after several heart attacks, his doctor advised him to be hospitalized immediately. Watson refused. "How can I spare the time? IBM is not a small company! Every day, so many things await my decisions. Without me . . ."

"Let's take a trip!" the doctor interrupted, and invited him to go for a drive.

After a while, they arrived at a cemetery. The doctor pointed to the graves one after another, saying, "One day, you and I are going to lie here forever. When you're gone, somebody else will take over your job. No matter who dies, the Earth keeps spinning. After you die, the business won't go under." Watson was silent.

The next day, one of the most powerful executives in the U.S. business community handed in his resignation to the board of directors and admitted himself to the hospital. After he was discharged, he went on to lead a life of adventure, traveling around the world. IBM didn't collapse; it's still a world-famous corporation.

Impermanence is certain, so it's important to be mentally prepared for change. No matter how unwilling we are to die, death will find us, and at that time, we have to leave behind even our most precious possession—our body.

The point is that we can survive loss, even if the loss is from death. At that time, there is no benefit in lamenting. The time to think about death is before it happens, so that when death comes, we can face it without regrets. Impermanence is constantly with us like our shadow. No matter how unwilling we are to die, death will visit us sooner or later. At that time, even our precious body must be left behind. We leave for the future life accompanied only by our karma, the actions we have accumulated over the course of our lives.

Some materialists are unwilling to accept this or think in this way. They proclaim that Buddhist study is escapism. In reality, the real escapism is to deny reincarnation and refuse to prepare for our next lives. This life will last several decades, if we are lucky, but the happiness and misery for thousands of years and lifetimes to come is determined by the karma of this life. Even if you are not fully convinced of this fact, how can you take the chance and blithely neglect such a possibility?

The fate of our future life is a central concern in Buddhism. Unfortunately most people have no idea about it. Even some Buddhists view Buddhism as merely a method to increase happiness in this present life through relaxation techniques. They never give a thought to the crucial matter of liberation or the happiness of future lives. Of course, it makes sense that people without such a belief ignore it. However, for people who for a long time claim to be Buddhists, and Mahayana Buddhists in particular, it is a serious problem to completely neglect future lives. It takes wisdom and courage to hold beliefs that are at odds with one's neighbors. Sometimes this world seems really like the story Chandrakirti told in his *Great Commentary on the Four Hundred Verses of the Middle Way*: When everybody in the whole country was crazy after drinking poisonous rain, the sober king was condemned by the masses as a lunatic because of his contrariness.

As it is, many people turn their backs whenever death is mentioned, and when told of the existence of future lives, reincarnation, and hells, they cover their ears and cry out, "Stop, stop! You're scaring me! Just let me be happy. I don't want to hear this." This is sheer self-deception. Clearly there is a long way to go before Buddhist beliefs are accepted as a mainstream view.

Wise people realize that to study the Dharma is in truth not passé. Whether we acknowledge it or not, past and future lives exist. Since they exist, how can we not have a long-term plan? Nowadays, in order to be carefree in their old age, many people open retirement accounts and purchase insurance policies. But have they thought to purchase the insurance of happiness after death?

Desire

Desire is endless. Many people believe that happiness can be found in houses, cars, fame, wealth, and status, so they keep themselves busy day after day chasing after such things. But how many people are really happy after getting what they want?

Once, there was a king who led a luxurious and extravagant life. He possessed plenty of treasure and many diversions, but he was still unhappy. He simply couldn't cheer himself up, and so he summoned the palace doctor. After a long examination, the doctor said, "Find the happiest person in the kingdom and wear his shirt. Then you will be happy." The king sent ministers to look everywhere for the happiest person, and finally they found an incurably happy person. However, the minister reported to the king that unfortunately there was no way to bring back his shirt.

The king was upset. "Why not?" he said, "I'm the king. How can I be refused a mere shirt?"

The minister replied, "The happy man is penniless. He has never even owned a shirt!" At that moment, the king truly recognized that happiness cannot be bought.

The fewer expectations you have, the happier you will be. If you expect a high standard of living and constantly pursue things, whether it is cell phones, clothes, houses, or cars, you will never feel content. This is because desire is endless. To live a comfortable and happy life, start by enriching your mind rather than blindly chasing after things. You will work yourself to death if you want everything. You will be happy in this life when you let go of desire.

Accepting Change

Nothing in this world is absolutely still. Everything is moving and changing. Because of impermanence, our happiness can't last forever—it can turn into suffering at any moment. Aryadeva's *Four Hundred Verses on the Middle Way* says,

> Anything impermanent is subject to falling apart,
> and falling apart is not happiness.
> Therefore what is impermanent
> is said to be suffering.

Once, there was a young and headstrong princess, pampered by her father the king. No matter what she wanted, the king would do whatever he could to fulfill her wishes. One day it was raining hard, and when the rain spattered on the puddles in the palace yard, it made lots of bubbles, which fascinated the princess so much that she told the king, "I want a garland of water bubbles to adorn my hair."

The king answered, "That's impossible."

The princess insisted, saying that if she didn't get what she wanted she would die. The king was frightened and convened all the artisans in the kingdom, commanding them to make a garland of water bubbles for the princess. Many young artisans were at their wit's end and extremely anxious for fear of the princess's disappointment.

One old craftsman claimed that he could do what she wanted on the condition that the princess be his consultant. The king was overjoyed and sent his daughter to the craftsman's workshop. The craftsman told the princess, "I can make the garland, but I can't tell nice water bubbles from ugly ones. Please bring me the ones you want, and then I will make them into a garland for you."

The princess happily agreed and went to choose her water bubbles, but even after trying a long time, she couldn't catch a single one. Exhausted, she turned around and ran into the palace to tell her father, "Water bubbles are very pretty, but when I catch them, they don't even last a moment. I don't want them anymore."

Suffering is rooted in clinging. The more deeply you realize the law of impermanence, the less overwhelming your suffering will be. If, for instance, you understand the impermanence of fame, its loss won't surprise you. If you understand the impermanence of affection, its failure won't make you desperate. If you make peace with the impermanence of life, you can recover from the devastation of a loved one's death.

At the time of the Buddha, a woman who was abandoned by her husband lost her child to a fatal illness shortly afterward. The woman was overcome with sorrow. With her child's corpse in her arms, she went to the Buddha and beseeched him out of his great compassion to bring the child back to life. The Buddha said, "First bring me a mustard seed from a household where nobody has died." The woman went from door to door, but not a single family had been spared from death. Finally she realized that people are bound to die and that everybody is equal in this way. She then began to make peace with her child's passing.

Su Shi said, "The moon waxes and wanes, dim and bright; likewise, people can become happy or sad, together or separated." This is the law of impermanence, and nobody can transcend it. If you understand this, your mind will open, and change won't drive you to despair.

Three Ways to Live

Once upon a time, three disciples, endlessly troubled by different problems and not knowing how to become happy, went to see the Chan master Wu De. The master began by asking them, "What have you lived for?"

The first one said, "In order not to die."

The second answered, "So that I can spend time with my children and grandchildren."

"For my wife and children," said the third.

The master replied, "None of you will be happy."

"Then how can we be happy?!" the three cried out.

The master asked, "What do you think can make you happy?"

The first man replied, "I think wealth can make me happy."

The second replied, "Love."

"Fame," said the third.

The master answered, "These thoughts will keep you unhappy forever. And even if you succeed in gaining wealth, love, and fame, you will still be beset by one afflictive emotion after another."

The three asked, "What should we do instead?"

The master said, "You must change your perspective. Instead of seeking wealth, give generously. Instead of searching for love, offer it to others. Instead of looking for fame, live your life in service to living beings. Only these can give you lifelong happiness."

The More Tightly You Cling to Something, the Sooner You Lose It

The happiness that most people pursue is just like holding sand: the tighter they hold it, the quicker it leaks away, and in the end they find their joy was mere dust. Wouldn't it be better to try your best, avoid dwelling on things, and let causes and conditions determine the extent of your success?

Once, a painter drew a dot on a blank piece of paper, had it framed, and asked people what its message was. There were a lot of opinions, but it was difficult to be sure what the artist had intended. In fact, the work's meaning was profound: if we grasp at only one thing, it's easy for us to neglect the space all around us. This is similar to when you're attached to someone. There are many things other than that person that can bring you happiness, but since you're fixated on that person alone, you feel the entire world leaves you behind when you can't get their affection. It's much better to appreciate the many sources of happiness in our environment and to avoid becoming attached to a single person.

Everything Will Pass

When you're respected for your fame and wealth, there's no cause to be arrogant because one day it will vanish. When you're penniless or reviled, there's no need to despair in agony either because that too will pass. Everything present will be in the past one day.

In ancient times, a queen had a dream in which somebody told her that as long as she kept one phrase in mind, anything she encountered in life could be dealt with. She was overjoyed, but when she awoke, she had forgotten the phrase. The desperate queen spent a fortune to have a huge diamond ring made. She then summoned the ministers and announced, "I will give this ring to anyone who can rediscover the phrase from my dream."

Two days later, an old minister came to her and said, "Your majesty! Please give me the diamond ring."

The queen asked, "Have you discovered the phrase?"

The old minister took the diamond ring away and had a phrase engraved on it. He then returned the ring to the queen and left without turning back. The queen looked at the ring and recognized the sentence from her dream, "Everything will pass!"

From then on, the queen firmly bore this motto in mind. No matter what happened in her life, she didn't worry too much because she understood that everything that happens to us—glory, disgrace, failure, wealth, fame, or gain—will eventually be in the past.

It's impossible to always have things go our way in life. To be indifferent to honor or disgrace, success or failure, is truly a transcendent state.

Cultivating Happiness

What is happiness? The ancient Chinese provided a possible answer when creating the characters for the word *happiness* (幸福). In the first character, the symbol for "land" is on the top and the symbol for "money" is at the bottom. In the second character, the symbol for "clothing" is on the left, the symbol for "one family" is on the upper right, and on the lower right is the symbol for "field." In other words, happiness is having land, money, clothing, food, and a family.

But is happiness really built on such things? Some people believe wealth can bring happiness, but I know a lot of rich people who aren't especially happy. Some believe affection can bring happiness and that happiness is meeting a congenial life companion with whom they can have a complete meeting of minds. Others believe happiness is good health. I know an old man who always makes offerings to the monastery and donations to charity. He does this without any other thought than for the safety and good health of his family. Happiness appears in different ways according to different values. What remains the same is that happiness is a sense of contentment established in your heart. So how do you get that?

Philosophers such as Socrates, Plato, and Hegel all agree that human beings should pursue happiness rationally. Happiness based on emotion is just a momentary experience, and like writing on water, it doesn't last. So let's explore the rational search for happiness. We can start by observing some qualities of what we normally call happiness.

Our feelings of happiness are transient.

Although we all wish that our happiness would stay forever, as time passes and we gradually get used to whatever it was that brought us happiness, the feeling of freshness disappears. For instance, sitting in our newly furnished house we may feel elated, but it won't take long for this feeling to begin to vanish. A man may feel he is the happiest person in the world when newly married, but years later, he might feel that marriage is tiresome, and he and his wife may even become like strangers. Our happiness is not everlasting or unchanging.

Happiness decreases every time the same source is obtained.

When we finally get something that we have wanted, we feel happy. But when we get that same thing a second time, the sense of happiness is not as great as before. Eventually the positive effect of the object wears off almost entirely.

The greater the effort, the greater the satisfaction.

We may feel incredibly happy when we obtain something that is very hard to get. For example, a Tibetan Buddhist who goes on pilgrimage to Lhasa by making prostrations the entire way and who endures tremendous hardship will be incredibly happy when she finally reaches her destination.

There is no happiness without yearning.

If we can't stop thinking about the pleasure we will get from something, then we will feel overjoyed when we finally get it. If we don't care for something, however, then it won't matter to us whether we get it or not. Cake is not a source of happiness for a man who doesn't like cake.

Happiness does not depend on the environment.

Suppose one person lives in a slum and another in a luxurious mansion. Just knowing this, we cannot say for certain which one is happier.

Happiness is easily overshadowed.

Say we are overcome with sorrow because of a tragedy in our lives. If at that moment, following a great effort, we finally get something we have been yearning for, it won't bring us much happiness.

Happiness as we normally think of it is dependent on external circumstances, but when we look rationally, we see very quickly that such happiness is not very reliable. If we never realize this and keep expecting external things to bring lasting contentment, then even after a lifetime of effort, we won't be satisfied, and that itself may even prevent our happiness from increasing.

This is because human desires are infinite. One Buddhist sutra says that even if a rain of jewels descended from the sky, and even if someone experienced all the wonderful sensory enjoyments in the world, if their desire were too strong, they would still be unable to feel content. I've met a lot of successful entrepreneurs. They're rich and famous, but they're still looking for more. Instead of feeling content, they feel anxious and empty, without even a taste of happiness.

Once, a rich man decided to travel in search of happiness. On his back he carried gold, silver, and jewels. After climbing a lot of mountains and crossing a lot of rivers, he still couldn't find any happiness. One day, despondent, he sat down by the side of the road. After a while, a farmer happened to pass by. The rich man asked him, "Could you please tell me where I can find happiness? I can't seem to find it anywhere, no matter how much I look."

The farmer put down the heavy firewood he was carrying, and wiping the sweat off his brow, he said, "Putting this down is happiness!" This was

76

a revelation for the rich man. He suddenly understood how to let go of his troubles, and that night, for the first time since he set off, he slept soundly.

There are so many things that we feel we can't put down. But when we do put them down, we begin to feel real happiness. With a contented mind, even if our life is not perfect and we can't completely reach our goals, we can still find lasting happiness.

4

The Value of Adversity

In this life's journey, every step you take
gains you the experience of that step,
whether it is the right step or the wrong.
A right step brings achievement,
and a wrong step gives a lesson.

Money Is Not a Substitute for Care

The Advantages of Failure

Whether an average person or someone in a position of power, each person in this world is striving to achieve something. Each hopes that everything will go smoothly, without setbacks, and without even the smallest frustration.

Yet failure has advantages. The Buddhist monk Hongyi said in his *Dream Image of the Ten Years in Southern Min*, "I wished only that what I engaged in failed. For only when things fail and are imperfect or incomplete do I feel ashamed and realize my lack of virtue and cultivation. That gives me the motivation to make efforts to earnestly mend my ways. No matter what, I hope I always fail, because only failure can trigger shame. If I become complacent because of my success, it will be disastrous."

I love this quote. Such thinking, while absurd to ordinary people, shows the modesty, great wisdom, and realization of this master.

In the *Treasury of Pith Instructions*, the great Tibetan master Longchenpa makes a profound statement: "Destroy self-attachment and always accept failure." Venerable Langri Tangpa also encouraged practitioners to "Let yourself take all loss and failure, and give away benefit and success." His and Hongyi's words share the same spirit. Bravely facing failure is the mark of a great person.

The Taiwanese writer Luo Lan said, "In this life's journey, every step you take gains you the experience of that step, whether it is the right step or the wrong. A right step brings achievement; a wrong step gives a lesson. If you are forced to make a detour or you lose your way, it is like entering a high mountain trail by mistake: Others may feel anxious and sorry for you, yet you collect rare flowers and fruits and see unusual birds

81

and beasts. Moreover, you learn a new route and become stronger and braver through this experience."

So you needn't fear failure. If you accept it with courage, you will taste its sweetness. An ancient proverb says, "Fortune and misfortune always follow each other."

Today's Suffering Was Sown Yesterday

Whatever you encounter in life comes from causes and conditions; nothing occurs for no reason.

When I was in Thailand, I read an ancient commentary on the *Dhammapada*. A story in it illustrates this point very well. A long time ago, a woman raised a hen. Every time the hen laid eggs and hatched her chicks, the woman would eat every one of them. As a result, the hen bore her a grudge and made a spiteful wish: "This vicious woman always eats my children. In future lives, I will eat her children!"

As it is said, karmic cause and effect, along with intention, never fails. Later, that woman took rebirth as a big hen, and the former hen took rebirth as a cat. Due to their karma, every time the big hen hatched her chicks, the cat would eat them. The big hen also became furious and made a spiteful aspiration: "This vicious cat always eats my children. I will do the same thing to her in future lives!"

After this pair of foes died, the cat was reborn as a doe, and the big hen was reborn as a leopard. The leopard would ruthlessly eat all the doe's little fawns. And so this tragedy of cyclic existence repeated endlessly.

At the time of Buddha Shakyamuni, the original hen was born as a demon and the original woman was born again as a woman. The demon went to eat the woman's children, but this time the woman held her children in her arms and, trembling with fear, ran to find the Buddha for refuge and protection.

Eventually, these two reached the Buddha, one chasing the other. The Buddha taught them with loving-kindness and compassion so that these foes from many lifetimes finally calmed down. Then the Buddha helped them understand their brutal past connections. "In this world," he told them, "hatred is never overcome by hatred but only by love. This is an eternal truth." Through his power, their feud finally ended, freeing them from their deadly cycle.

In cyclic existence, this pattern of retaliation happens all the time. When you encounter malice and misfortune, you must be vigilant, keeping in mind that this is merely the ripening of your previous negative actions. Never return hate with hate and fuel the cycle of retaliation. Otherwise, the tragedy of the hen and the cat will be reenacted endlessly.

Many people have little tolerance. Just a few offensive words—to say nothing of actual physical harm—can send some into a rage. Patience is an essential virtue. Han Shan said, "In this world of boundless cares and troubles, patience and meekness are a wonderful remedy."

It is said that the Buddhist monk Budai was an emanation of Buddha Maitreya and that when others cursed him, he would burst into laughter and applaud them. When he was beaten by others with a stick, he would lie down immediately to save their energy. When others spat in his face, he wouldn't wipe it off but would let it dry naturally. Most of us can't act like this. Forget about being spat on—when someone washing his hands splashes water on our shoes, we lose our temper and scold him!

If you're irritated by whatever you see or hear and view everything with cynicism, it's exhausting! The best approach is to let go of any conflict as soon as possible. Even if you are abused, humiliated, and slandered in public, the armor of patience is the best defense. "One moment of patience returns peace and calm. One conciliatory step opens up a space as vast as the ocean and the sky."

The Practice of Patience

The patience of not returning harm, of not giving in to hatred, is incredibly difficult to cultivate. The *Way of the Bodhisattva* says, "There's no transgression like hatred, and no fortitude like patience." Among all the wrongdoings, nothing is as frightening as hatred; among all the austerities, nothing is more difficult than patience.

In a previous lifetime, Buddha Shakyamuni was born as a sage whose name meant "power of patience." He made the aspiration to never harbor hatred toward sentient beings. To destroy his practice, a demon manifested a thousand people who cursed the sage with malicious language, slandered him, and humiliated him with vulgar language in public. These people constantly provoked him, but no matter what treatment he received, the sage never showed an angry look or thought of retaliating. He never even said things like "What on earth have I done wrong?" He only quietly made the aspiration "By this merit of practicing patience, may all sentient beings reach unsurpassable enlightenment. When I reach buddhahood, I will come to liberate these people first!"

As a follower of the Buddha, always remind yourself of this story. Understand that hatred is directly contradictory to loving-kindness and compassion. The primary goal of the Mahayana is to help sentient beings, but once hatred has arisen, this goal vanishes, and you no longer want to benefit sentient beings and instead seek to harm them. This is completely contrary to the Mahayana teachings. So among all transgressions, nothing is worse than hatred. This is easy to understand but not easy to actually put into practice once we are provoked.

I heard a story about a Japanese Zen master known for his patience. A local girl had an affair and gave birth to a son. Fearing that her Buddhist parents would berate her, the girl told her parents it was the master's son. She thought she wouldn't be scolded by her parents because they always held the master in high regard. Her parents believed her and took the newborn baby to the master. Once there, they started cursing him: "You, who pretend to be a monk, have soiled the Buddhadharma! We didn't see your vile nature and were deceived by you. We never believed you could do something like this. You're worse than an animal. This is your son—take him!"

The master said calmly, "Really?" and took the baby in his arms. The parents felt justified in their reproach and spread the story around. Before long, everyone had heard and gave the master dirty looks wherever he went.

The master, holding the weak infant, went to ask for milk from a family with another newborn baby. They said, "If it wasn't for the sake of the poor baby, you wouldn't get anything!"

Day after day, the girl suffered tremendous guilt. Finally, she couldn't bear to see people treating the master unfairly and confessed to her parents what had happened. Ashamed, the parents went to confess to the master. The master replied in the same way, "Really?"

If this happened to us, would we be so calm?

Patience Should Be Tested

After working to cultivate patience for a while, some people think they have succeeded and become complacent. Don't be satisfied too early—first test it!

Once, there was a quick-tempered old man. To avoid getting angry, he had the words "Infinite Patience Realm" hung in his living room to remind him to be patient. After a while, he believed he had become very successful in cultivating patience. He felt so confident that he bragged about it. One day, in order to test him, a beggar came to his living room and with feigned innocence asked, "How do you read these three words?"

"Infinite Patience Realm," he replied with a smile.

"Oh, Infinite Patience Realm," the beggar repeated and walked out.

A moment later, the beggar came back and asked again, "I'm so sorry! I forgot what you said. Could you please repeat it?"

The old man said, a little sharply, "Infinite Patience Realm!"

"Right, right! Thank you!"

A little while later, he came back and asked the same question. The old man yelled, "Can't you remember just three words? It's Infinite Patience Realm!"

The beggar laughed and said, "Actually, it's Limited Patience Realm!"

Patience is the most difficult practice because anger is easily triggered by even slightly unpleasant words or experiences.

Another story makes the same point. A general became tired of battle after serving in combat for a long time. He went out of his way to visit the Chan master Zong Gao and asked to be ordained. The master said, "No hurry! Wait and see."

The general pleaded, "I can let go of everything right now. My wife, children, and family all pose no problem, for I have abandoned attachment to them. Please shave my head now!"

The master advised, "Let's talk about it later." The general had no choice but to go home.

One day, the general got up early and ran to the temple to perform prostrations to the statue of the Buddha. Master Zong Gao saw him and asked, "General, why have you come to perform prostrations so early?"

The general said, "To put out the fire in my heart, I got up early to pay homage to the Buddha."

The master joked, "You left your house so early. Aren't you afraid your wife may take advantage of your absence to seduce another man?"

The general became angry and cursed, "You monster! Your words are disgusting!"

The master burst into laughter and said, "Only by slightly blowing at coals, the flame of anger blazes up again. Can a reaction like that be called letting go?"

This story reminds us never to boast too soon. Even if you think that you can let something go, until you have tested yourself with adversity, you can't say that you've succeeded.

The Eight Worldly Concerns

The four pairs of gain and loss, happiness and pain, praise and criticism, and hope and fear are called the *eight worldly concerns*. People want the positive four and reject the negative four. For instance, we are happy if we are praised but get angry if we are criticized. Our mood fluctuates according to these eight concerns, so we must try by all means to let them go. Of course, everyone can say that they don't care about these things, but most people can't actually manage to control their day-to-day moods. Since we are blown to and fro by these eight concerns throughout our lives, they are also called the *eight winds*.

The story of Su Dongpo is a good example. When he was sent to take office in Guazhou above the Yangzi River, his friend the Chan master Fo Yin was at the Gold Mountain temple on the opposite bank. They often met to discuss Chan and the path.

One day, Su Dongpo had a powerful experience in meditation and immediately composed a verse: "I pay homage to the supreme ones in the sky, whose brilliant rays radiate in the billionfold universe; not being blown by the winds of the eight worldly concerns, you sit steadily on the golden lotus." This poem appeared to praise the buddhas and bodhisattvas, but in fact it was to imply that he would no longer be blown by the eight winds. He was very satisfied with himself and cheerfully asked his servant to send it to Master Fo Yin for validation. After reading it, the master commented with two words and asked the servant to send it back.

Su Dongpo was confident that the master would offer some sort of praise and couldn't wait to see his reply. When it arrived, all it said was, "Break wind!" Flushed with anger, he immediately took a boat across the river, ready for an argument. To his surprise, the master was waiting for him at the front gate of the temple. As soon as he reached the master, Su Dongpo confronted him: "I see you as my friend and confidant. You don't need to acknowledge my realization, but how can you be so disrespectful?"

The master replied calmly, "What did I say?"

He showed the two words to the master.

Taking a look at it, the master burst into laughter and said, "Not blown by the eight winds but blown across the river by a fart."

Su Dongpo was smart. He understood immediately and felt ashamed.

Worldly people are easily affected by the eight winds. It's only after emptiness is directly experienced that all the illusions can completely disappear. The great Longchenpa said in *Finding Comfort and Ease in the Nature of Mind*, "When space-like emptiness is examined, joy and worry, gain and loss, virtue and vice don't exist." I've heard many Buddhist practitioners say, "Gain and loss don't exist." Yet every day, as though possessed, they strive to gain and not to lose. This means that they are still entangled in the game of gain, loss, and worrying.

Even before you realize emptiness, if you can understand that everything in the world is transient like smoke and clouds, you can eliminate the major attachments, no longer be affected by external objects, and reach the state described like this: "Indifferent to honor and disgrace, you watch with comfort the blooming and withering of flowers in the yard; unconcerned about leaving or staying, with ease you view the clouds rolling and unfolding in the sky."

Understanding Karma

In this diverse world, some people have abundant wealth and great power, while others, nose to the grindstone, barely eke out a living. Some people are handsome and elegant, while others are ugly and constantly subjected to scorn. Some people live a happy and satisfied life, while others experience intense suffering throughout their entire life. Buddhism says these different fates are not caused by a god and they are not random; they are the fruits of previous actions.

Some people may ask, "If karma is true, why is it that some people don't experience positive consequences even after doing good deeds, while others don't experience negative results even after committing negative actions?" This is actually easy to answer. It's just like when farmers sow seeds in the spring—the plants can't bear fruit immediately. Similarly, in between the sowing and the reaping of a positive or negative action, a period of time is required. However, karma ultimately never fails. As long as the cause is created, the effect will ripen sooner or later.

Others complain that the more virtuous deeds they do, the poorer their business and the greater their loss, but this is not the case. Their expectation of instant results is as impossible as for farmers to sow barley or wheat today and reap it tomorrow. The Indian master Nagarjuna said that unlike cutting the body with a knife, which causes bleeding immediately, karma doesn't bear its fruit right away. But when the causes meet the appropriate conditions, the effect of previous virtue and vice will inevitably arise.

A Buddhist sutra says, "To understand the causes from a previous life, look at your experience in this life. To learn what effects you will experience in your future life, watch what you do in this present life." You reap what you sow. Many people are curious about their previous lives, but there is actually no need to ask others. You can find the answer by just looking at this life.

It is not just ancient people who believe this. Many modern people are also convinced. Once, I was sick and receiving a massage every day following my doctor's advice. After a while, the masseuse and I became very familiar. He was very good at his job, and we passed the time in conversation. One time he told me sincerely, "Buddhism always talks about cause and effect. I find it really makes sense. I must have done some negative action in a previous life, so I am blind this life. However, I must have done some positive action, so I have such a skill and can lead a carefree life. Cause and effect really ring true for me."

I pondered his words for a long time. In this world, many able-bodied people are not as good as this blind man. Unaware of cause and effect, they wantonly commit negative actions, blame all their adversity on others, and do not know that all the virtue and cruelty they experience are created by themselves. If everybody has as much conviction in cause and effect as this blind masseuse, there would be more kindness and less fearfulness in this world.

Virtue Is the Best Protection

Once, I heard a lama lamenting, "It seems as if nobody is thriving these days. Today, this person is not doing well: something wrong in his family. Tomorrow, that person is not doing well: getting frustrated in his job. But if they always harm others for the sake of themselves, how can they expect to do well? No matter how many deities they pray to, it is useless."

In my part of the world, Buddhists make offerings to bodhisattvas and other enlightened beings to create positive karma, and they supplicate protectors for aid and safety. I believe that buddhas and bodhisattvas do indeed have the power to give blessings and that Dharma protectors and deities also have mighty power. But the more important question to ask is what kind of person are you? Even many Buddhists ignore this question. No matter who you are, whether you are Buddhist or not, if you appreciate kindness, return it, and sincerely believe in cause and effect, people will respect and help you, and your mind will be more at ease. Not only that, but Dharma protectors and deities will help you too. For what pleases the buddhas most is for us to practice the golden rule and develop our good qualities.

Once, Master Yin Guang told a story. Toward the end of the Ming dynasty, Li Zicheng led an armed uprising in which many common people lost their families and became destitute and homeless. A man, whose surname was Yuan, lost his son while fleeing the turmoil, and so he wished to take a concubine to have another heir. Mr. Yuan brought a woman home but found she was crying heartbrokenly. He asked her the reason, and she replied, "We are too poor to have any food; my husband was going to kill himself because of starvation, so I decided to sell myself to save my husband. Now, in hindsight, I realized our good fortune. We have a very good relationship, but now, we have to be separated. How can I not be so heartbroken?" After hearing this, Mr. Yuan felt sorrowful. At daybreak, he sent the woman home with a hundred taels of silver and advised them to make a living by starting a small business.

The couple was so appreciative and planned to find a good woman for Mr. Yuan to have an heir, but they could not find one. Later, they met a good-looking boy who was down on his luck, and they thought, "Before we find a good woman, let's first send this boy to attend Mr. Yuan." Hence, they paid for the boy to go to Mr. Yuan. After repeated scrutiny, Mr. Yuan recognized that this boy was actually his son, lost for many years. Good fortune follows the virtuous.

Only a buddha can truly know what action produces what result. But as long as we consistently cultivate virtuous thoughts and deeds, as long as we create merit, fortunate results will appear in various ways. A lot of people pursue fame, position, and wealth, but without merit, it's just like trying to grow a tree on the North Pole. The tree of success can only take root and flourish in the soil of our positive thoughts and actions, in the merit of kindness. The success enjoyed by people is the result of their virtuous deeds in previous lives. Without the cause of virtuous deeds, the effect of fortune would never come about. If you want to pursue fame, gain, or security, understand this and always cultivate kind thoughts and actions. In this way, fortune will grow naturally—if not in this life, then in a future one. For that is the law of karma. Pleasant experiences inevitably grow from virtuous seeds, and suffering comes from nonvirtue. Once you fully and deeply recognize the truth of this, you will avoid negative actions even if your life lies in the balance.

5

Meditation in Speech

Frogs croak day and night,
but nobody pays them any attention.
Roosters, who only crow at dawn,
rouse everyone from bed.
The point is not to speak a lot
but to speak at the right time.

Negative Speech

A major cause of pushing other people away is negative speech. Some people say whatever they like with no thought of others. In a rage, many will speak without restraint. But even if they realize their mistake afterward, what has been said can't be taken back. So it's better to learn how to avoid saying regrettable things in the first place!

The ancients said, "The wound cut by a sharp blade is easy to recover from, but the wound aroused by malicious words is not easily healed." When the body is injured, the wound can heal in time, but when the mind is hurt, the victim usually aggravates the wound and compounds the injury. When slandered in public, people immediately respond with an angry or horrified look. The quick-tempered return like for like on the spot. Others may not retaliate right away but cultivate the hatred in their mind, "irrigating and fertilizing" it every day, and letting the seed of hatred root and germinate gradually but firmly.

It is vital we practice mindfulness of speech.

Promises

Reliable people don't make promises easily, but once they do, they keep them. The Chinese saying "One promise is worth a thousand measures of gold" originally comes from a story in the *Records of the Grand Historian*.

Toward the end of the Qin dynasty, in the Chu area, there lived a man named Ji Bu who attached great importance to promises. Once he promised something, no matter how difficult it was, he would do everything he could to fulfill it. The people in Chu still say, "It's better to get a promise from Ji Bu than a thousand taels of gold."

Confucius said in the *Analects*, "The ancient sages didn't easily make promises and were ashamed if they failed to keep them." When Confucius's student Zeng Can was educating his children, he was as strict with himself as he was with them. Once, his wife was planning to go to the fair, and their son started crying to persuade her to take him with her. She didn't want to bring him and said, "You stay home and play as much as you like. When I get back, I will kill a pig and cook it for you." Hearing this, the son was delighted and stopped crying. She only said this to fool him and soon forgot about it. However, Zeng Can went ahead and killed a pig for him.

After returning from the fair and discovering what had happened, Zeng Can's wife became angry and said, "I only said that because I couldn't think of another way to put him off. How could you take it literally?"

Zeng Can replied, "Children shouldn't be tricked. He will only imitate us. Fooling him today is teaching him to lie in the future." As parents, you must keep in mind the long-term effects of your child-rearing choices. If you lie to your children, they will learn that it is acceptable to lie, no matter what you teach them with your words.

Once, when I was building a school, a benefactor who had heard that I had a shortage of funds came forward and said, "I promised a large amount of money to another master for a construction project, but it's not working out. Wouldn't it be better for me to transfer the money to you to help you build your school?" I said, "Since you have already promised him, you shouldn't change your mind. I will find other ways to raise the funds." Even though he had faith in me, I didn't think his offer was fair because it would mean breaking his promise.

There's another Chinese saying: "Don't promise anything when infatuated. Don't reply to letters when enraged." In other words, don't promise to give anything to anyone when you're feeling overjoyed, and when you're extremely angry, don't send messages of any kind! People with genuine wisdom never make promises in the heat of the moment; otherwise it's very easy to get into a dilemma.

Your Words Can Haunt You

To make fun of someone's physical attributes may seem harmless, but such speech can be extremely painful for the recipient. Not only that, it may ripen back upon you in ways you don't expect.

A story in the *Sutra of the Foolish and the Wise* about the monk whose name means Best Honey demonstrates the consequences of this. At the time of the Buddha, the monk Best Honey obtained freedom from suffering very quickly, and so the other monks asked the Buddha what past-life causes and conditions made this possible. "One time," the Buddha answered, "I was on my alms round, and I came across a monkey who offered me some honey. When I accepted it, the monkey was so overjoyed he scampered about and inadvertently fell into a deep pit and died. That monkey took rebirth as a human being, the present monk Best Honey."

"Why was he a monkey in previous life?" asked the monks.

The Buddha replied, "In the age of the previous Buddha, Kashyapa, Best Honey was a young monk. One day, he spied an enlightened monk jumping across a river, and he mocked the other monk, saying he was like a monkey. Because of this unpleasant remark, Best Honey was born as a monkey five hundred times." It goes without saying you should avoid mocking the handicaps of others, but it is wise as well to avoid comparing them to a monkey, a cow, a dog, or a pig.

When teaching the *Thirty-Seven Practices of a Bodhisattva*, the Seventeenth Karmapa said that the First Karmapa Dusum Khyenpa had been born as a monkey for five hundred lifetimes due to calling a monk a monkey at the time of the Buddha Kashyapa. Afterward, when born as Dusum Khyenpa, he looked like a monkey, and before he took ordination, his lover had left him because of his unusual appearance. This was how the mind of renunciation arose in him.

Though negative words are only words, they have an impact on us. It's better to be mindful and watch what you say. Sakya Pandita said, "Give up saying cruel words to anyone, even enemies. Otherwise, even if you're able to render them speechless and embarrassed, the curse you throw out will eventually ripen on you, just like echoes in a valley."

Skillful Means

Buddha Shakyamuni gave teachings in accordance with the different capacities of his audiences. It is said that he developed 84,000 Dharma teachings, each of which is like a specific medicine that can cure a corresponding mental ailment.

The Buddha had ten great disciples in his entourage. Among them, Venerable Purna was considered the best at teaching Dharma because he was very good at choosing a topic that suited his audience. If he were talking to a doctor, he would say, "You doctors can cure physical diseases and relieve pains, but do you have methods to cure desire, hatred, and ignorance?"

The doctor would usually reply, "I don't. Do you?"

He would answer, "The Buddha's teachings are like medicines that can purify mental defilements. The three trainings of discipline, concentration, and wisdom are like a panacea that can cure the mental diseases of desire, hatred, and ignorance."

Similarly, if he were talking to the local authorities, he would say, "You can punish criminals, but can you prevent people from committing a crime?"

The authorities usually answered, "Although there are laws, we can't always stop people from breaking them."

He would then say, "If people study and follow the Dharma, which severs the roots of negative deeds, crime will disappear."

Likewise, if he met a farmer working in a field, he would say, "You can feed the body by plowing the field and planting crops, but would you like to learn how to plow the field of merit and nourish wisdom?"

The farmer might answer, "Yes," or "What are they?"

He would then say, "Having faith in the Buddhadharma, respecting monks and nuns, taking care of the sick, being enthusiastic about charity and loyal to your parents, rejecting nonvirtue and advocating virtue among neighbors, and giving up killing—these are the best ways to plow the field of merit."

In this way, he always taught people according to their backgrounds so that they could easily understand him no matter who they were. If you're not motivated by self-interest, choosing the words that best suit your audience is not manipulative, it's skillful. Mastery of this can help you to achieve maximum impact with the least effort.

Knowing When to Speak

An old saying goes, "Illness comes through the mouth; an eager tongue will always cause misfortune." No matter who you are, it's important to be careful with your words. Some people keep quiet all the time in fear of offending others, but sometimes it is important to speak up. Other people talk all day just because they like to argue and gossip. Not a single one of their remarks is useful. When the conversation moves toward the faults of another, their eyes sparkle with excitement, but once meaningful subjects take over the conversation, their eyes glaze over and they start to doze.

We should adjust the way we talk to the character of the person we are with. With moral and sincere people, we can speak directly and even scold them a little. With those who try to push our buttons, who like to exaggerate or distort the truth, or who pry gossip from us and then make up stories, it's best not to talk much unless you want trouble. A lot of people don't understand this principle and end up in hot water again and again. If they said only what needed to be said when it needed to be said and nothing more, they would be much better off.

Mipham Rinpoche said, "People with improper speech, like crows, upset everyone." Crows caw all day long, and the sound itself is considered a bad omen in some cultures. Similarly, people who talk improperly or incessantly are always upsetting others.

When leaving Tibet, the great master Padmasambhava told his disciples, "It's not easy for those who like talking nonsense to hide what they think. What they joke about can be misunderstood as truth, and the truth they tell can be mistaken for a joke. For this reason, easy things become difficult. So, disciples, it's best to hold your tongue!"

Similarly, the Chan master Wumen Huikai, author of the *Gateless Gate*, called himself "the silent old man." A poem he wrote says,

> Well acquainted with the sight of the moon
> yet weary of moving my tongue:
> I've experienced everything in the world,
> yet I only nod my head.
> Say not that this old man is out of tricks,
> let alone that I have no comfort and ease.

In the *Mozi* one of Mozi's disciples asks, "Is it good to talk a lot?"

Mozi answers, "Toads and frogs croak day and night, but nobody pays attention to them, even when their mouths and tongues are dried out. Roosters, who only crow at dawn, shake everything under heaven and get everyone out of bed. What use is talking a lot? The point is to speak at the right time."

The Power of Pleasant Speech

When communicating with others, language is vital. When we are gentle with our words, wrongs aren't created and merits are accumulated. If someone is hurt by something you say, the wound may take a long time to heal. As Mencius says, "One kind remark can make people feel warm in the severest of winters; malicious words can make people feel cold even in summer."

Some believe that harsh words are more powerful because they help to advance some goal. In truth, this belief is mistaken. There is an ancient fable about this. The North Wind and the Sun once competed to see who would be able to remove a traveler's cloak. The North Wind displayed its might first, blowing fiercely. The harder it blew, however, the more tightly the man wrapped the cloak around himself. The Sun then took its turn. As the wind stopped and the sun came out, the man felt so warm that he had to take the cloak off.

Pleasant words are like the Sun, while harsh words are like the North Wind. Fools believe that in order to succeed, harsh words must be used, while the wise can handle things perfectly with gentle speech.

Besides using gentle words, it's critical that you also make your meaning clear. The *Way of the Bodhisattva* says, "When talking, I should make the words pleasant, the meaning clear, and the content relevant." Some people rattle on for a long time without anyone knowing what to make of it. When talking, besides considering others' feeling, be as clear as you can!

6

Parents

The heart of a mother is like water,
while the heart of a son is like stone.

Sacrifice

Today many people keep their parents at arm's length, saying they're too busy with their work and other commitments. Unconcerned with their parents' aging and loneliness, they forget how selflessly their parents raised them despite all kinds of hardship.

A Tibetan saying goes, "The heart of a mother is like water, while the heart of a son is like stone." Sadly, children at times can become indifferent to their parents. Yet even if the children are already forty or fifty years old, many parents still can't let go of their concern for their children.

Think of your parents and check your conscience. Do you really fulfill your filial obligations to them? The Chinese character "filial" (孝) is made up of the characters for "old" on top and "offspring" below. This gives us a sense of the original meaning: offspring should uphold or support their parents.

How many people do this these days? Many people ignore their parents, and when their parents call them, they don't answer and carry on with their own business. Even if they do answer, they often do so impatiently. But it's critical that you try to help your parents as they age and become vulnerable.

During the Tang dynasty, there was a monk who was an only child and took full responsibility for caring for his mother. At one point he was penniless, and to prevent his old mother from going hungry, he pawned his monastic robes to buy rice to feed her. Later he wrote a poem:

> Frost falls on the reed flowers, tears wet my clothes.
> My old mother is no longer leaning on the doorframe.
> Last May, in the rainy season,
> I pawned my robes to bring rice home.

It's clear from the biographies of past masters that they still had close connections with their parents and that it didn't interfere with their realization. These days, however, some monks and nuns have very little connection with their parents, which is a mistake. It wasn't just Confucius who advocated taking care of our parents; this is also a fundamental practice in Buddhism. A number of sutras expound the difficulty of returning the kindness of our parents and how we should strive to do so. In Buddhism, parents are viewed as "strong fields," which means that if we commit negative actions against them, the result will be immense.

Monks and nuns are even allowed to use the money offered to them to feed their parents. At the time of the Buddha, there was a monk whose parents were very poor. He wanted to offer them food and clothing, so he asked the Buddha for permission. The Buddha called together the assembly of monks and told them, "Even though you are ordained, you should still give to your parents."

He also said, "Buddhahood relies completely on the kindness of parents. To learn the path, diligently take care of them." So whatever kind of person you are, never forget to return your parents' kindness.

No Time to Waste

Once, when Confucius was walking with some of his disciples, they heard a mournful cry in the distance. When they arrived, they found a man called Gao Yu dressed in a sackcloth with a sickle and pick in his hands. He was weeping by the roadside. Confucius asked, "Why are you crying? Has someone died?"

Gao Yu said, "I made three mistakes! In my youth, out of curiosity I traveled abroad and put my parents in second place. That was my first mistake. Later, to fulfill my dreams, I served our emperor and didn't serve my parents well. That was my second mistake. Then, staying close to my friends, I neglected my family. That was my third mistake. Now, having finally understood the need to return my parents' kindness, they are no longer alive. I became filled with intense remorse and couldn't help crying."

Hearing this, Confucius told his disciples, "You should take this as a lesson!"

No matter who we are, the kindness of our parents in giving birth to us and nurturing us is really inconceivable. The *Classic of Poetry* says, "My poor parents! To give birth to me, you have endured all kinds of hardship. The kindness I should return is as immense as the sky." So while your parents are still alive, be kind to them, take care of them, and don't wait to cry in remorse like Gao Yu!

Money Is Not a Substitute for Care

Some people send their parents money every month, believing they have fulfilled their filial duties. But this is not sufficient. Confucius said, "Nowadays, those who feed their parents are called devoted, but their dogs and horses are well fed too. Without respect, what is the difference?" When nurturing you, your parents didn't only give you material goods but also immense love. Therefore, to return this profound kindness, be genuinely concerned about them, keeping them in mind all the time, just as parents keep us in mind all the time.

In ancient China, Huang Xiang was well known for his filial devotion. When he was nine years old, his mother died. From then on, he took even better care of his father, charging himself with all the housework. Every night in winter, for fear of his father catching a cold, he would get into the cold bed first. He would only help his father into bed once the covers were warmed up. In the summer, he would cool the mat with a fan every night to help his father fall asleep quickly. This kind of care is what children should aspire toward.

Although financial support is necessary, giving parents emotional comfort is critical, too. They often feel lonely and neglected in their old age, so we should comfort them and try to cheer them up. When we were born, we couldn't feed or clothe ourselves—it was our parents who made sacrifices to raise us. Then they concerned themselves with our education, work, and relationships. Now we have grown up, but our parents have aged. If we aren't concerned with them, it is unconscionable!

Some people aren't concerned enough about their parents. They act as if their parents had never cared about them. Of course, this may also be related to the education they received from their parents. For example, if when a family eats together the parents dote on the children, always serving them first, saying things like, "You're such a little darling!" this is actually not right. At meals when the extended family is together, children should first show respect to their grandparents and then to their father and mother. Educated little by little in this way, they will gradually become respectful toward their elders.

During the Three States period, there was a man called Lu Ji. Once, when he was only six years old, he was invited to visit the warlord Yuan Su. Yuan Su asked a servant to offer him some tangerines. Lu Ji didn't eat any and instead stealthily hid some in his clothes. Later, when asking permission to leave, he bowed to Yuan Su, and three tangerines rolled out from his tunic. Yuan Su burst into laughter, "Haven't you had enough? You have to take some home?"

"They looked so nice that it seemed a shame to eat them myself. I wanted to take some home for my mother." Yuan Su was very surprised and thought that it was really admirable for a six-year-old child to be so self-disciplined and dutiful to his elders.

So be kind to your parents, just like the little Lu Ji, and always keep them in mind.

Seeing Your Parents as Bodhisattvas

With a little learning, some people become proud. Whenever their parents try to teach them something, they give a look of disdain and say, "What do you know?" Some even lose their temper and say, "Stop telling me what to do!" This undoubtedly hurts their parents. Since parents have sincere love for their children, their instructions must be of value. Recognize and appreciate their sacrifices and hard work on your behalf. Especially when parents scold you when you make a mistake, listen humbly. It's said, "The more profound the love, the more stern the scolding."

In ancient times, there was a man called Yang Pu who was very much loved by his parents. As he grew up and his parents got older, he didn't like listening to them anymore and found their conversation boring.

One day he thought of becoming a monk. He heard that Master Wuji had attained realization, so he said goodbye to his parents and set out by himself to visit the master and seek the Dharma.

When he found Master Wuji, he said, "I'd like to be your disciple and learn the Dharma."

The master replied, "You'd better learn directly from the Buddha and bodhisattvas."

"I would like to see the Buddha," Yang Pu said, "but where is the Buddha?"

The master told him, "It's simple! Go home now, and when you see someone with a blanket over their shoulders wearing their shoes on the wrong feet, that is an emanation of the Buddha." After hearing this, Yang Pu was eager to find the Buddha and left for home.

It was already midnight when he arrived. He knocked at the gate and called to his mother to open the door. His mother was so glad to hear that her son had returned that she jumped out of bed, and without bothering to put on her clothes, she quickly put a blanket over her shoulders. In a hurry to open the door, she didn't even notice that she had put her shoes on the wrong feet. When he saw his mother with a blanket over her shoulders wearing her shoes on the wrong feet, he remembered the master's words. All of the encouragement and forgiveness his mother had given him came back to him, and he saw his mother in a new light.

No matter how poor an education your parents may have, their life experience is much richer than yours, and what they say is for your sake, so lend an attentive ear. When he was little, Mencius was tired of studying and didn't like to go to school. Once, he snuck home from school early and found his mother weaving a piece of cloth. Seeing her son home early, she didn't say a word but broke her shuttle, entirely ruining an almost-done piece of cloth. A faithful son, Mencius kneeled down immediately and asked, "Why did you do that?"

His mother said, "Studying is not just a two-day affair. It's just like weaving cloth: you must start with a single string, and then, inch by inch, an entire piece of cloth can be woven. Only when an entire piece of cloth is woven can it be used to make clothes. Likewise, if you study without perseverance, give up in the middle, and feel satisfied with a little learning, how can you succeed in the future?"

Mencius understood the lesson. From then on he studied wholeheart-edly and never played truant again. Later he was so erudite that he became the "second sage," and in learning he was second only to Confucius.

Despite the poor education of some elders, they have survived immense suffering and have the flexibility and skills to deal with people. When dealing with problems in your life, consult your parents. Their instructions and advice are of great help. Otherwise, acting against their advice, it's easy to find yourself in trouble soon afterward.

Speak Gently to Your Parents

Often parents, as they get older, start acting like children. If your parents' behavior is improper, like gambling, drinking, or quarreling every day, advise them gently and avoid sharp words or a stern attitude. Once, I heard a young man say proudly, "Today, my father made a big mistake, so I chastised him fiercely." Even if his father were wrong, what he did wasn't appropriate. Parents are elders, so we should advise them with gentle words. If due to different perspectives your parents reject your ideas, express your reasons tactfully.

In ancient times, there was a child called Shun Yuanjue who was respectful to his elders from an early age. His father, however, was unfaithful to his grandfather. One day, his father abruptly put his grandfather, who was old, sick, and weak, in a basket, planning to leave him deep in the mountains to live out his final days there. Shun Yuanjue pleaded with his father and kneeled on the floor crying, but he couldn't make his father change his mind.

Suddenly, Shun Yuanjue had an idea. Wiping away the tears, he said, "You have decided to discard grandfather, and I can't do anything about it. But can you do me a favor and please bring the basket back?"

Puzzled, the father asked, "What will you do with it?"

"When you are old, I will use it to discard you," he replied.

Alarmed, the father said, "How can you say that?"

Shun Yuanjue answered, "I am just trying to follow your example." Shocked into understanding, the father immediately brought the old man inside and took very good care of him from then on.

Therefore, even if your parents are incorrect and by nature difficult to communicate with, you should gradually induce them to give up their wrong actions with skillful means and avoid using sharp words or embarrassing them. If they refuse your advice, keep asking them with respect and a sincere attitude. After repeated admonishment, wise parents will eventually accept it. If you persuade your parents gently when they are mistaken, it's much more likely that they will change their minds. That way their honor is preserved, and your filial duty is fulfilled.

7

Bliss in Birth, Old Age, Sickness, and Death

*To fear aging while wishing for a long life
is the view of fools.*

SAKYA PANDITA

Prepare Early for Death

Yogi Chowang was one of the principal disciples of Dakpo Rinpoche, and he is widely acknowledged in Tibet for his great accomplishments. Once, a practitioner from Kham went out of his way to pay a visit to this master. After offering the yogi a piece of cloth, he asked for a teaching. The yogi taught him nothing. After repeated requests, the yogi held his hand and said sincerely, "I will die, so will you! I will die, so will you! I will die, so will you!" and then told him, "There are no other teachings than this. I swear no instruction is more supreme than this."

Some might think, "How can this be a profound teaching? Even I can teach 'I will die, so will you!'" But this practitioner from Kham had great faith and thought, "What the guru taught makes sense. Eventually the guru will pass from this life, and I will also die one day. When I die, I can't take my body with me, let alone anything else. I should recognize impermanence and give up fixating on this life." From then on he practiced diligently according to this instruction and achieved great spiritual accomplishments.

As practitioners, we must always remember death. The great master Yin Guang had the word "death" written in large letters in his shrine room and always exhorted people, saying, "Human life is impermanent, as fleeting as a lightening flash," and, "Life is short. How long is a human life? Once one breath is not followed by another, it's already the afterlife." We can see the importance great masters placed on death.

In order to be free from birth and death, great practitioners of the past endured all kinds of hardship. With firm determination and fearless diligence, through sincere practice day and night, they finally recognized the nature of mind. It's a pity when people haggle over every ounce and rack their brains over every worldly concern yet ignore the bigger issues of birth and death as if the Lord of Death will overlook them. This is as self-deceiving as trying to steal a bell and, instead of muffling it, plugging one's ears to stop the sound!

From beginningless time, due to our dualistic attachment, we have lost sight of our original nature. Since our intrinsic luminous nature has been obscured by ignorance, we are perpetually tossed about in the ocean of birth and death. Without realizing the path, it's difficult to overcome the obstacles of birth, old age, sickness, and death. In order to recognize in ourselves that luminous nature that is permanently free from birth and death, we have to make strenuous effort.

There's a saying: "The sharpness of a sword comes from grinding; the fragrance of the plum blossom comes from extreme cold." Only by letting go of everything, remembering death regularly, and practicing without laziness can the intrinsic fragrance of enlightenment be revealed.

Practicing Later in Life

After studying the Dharma, many older people find genuine spiritual sustenance and a greater sense of certainty about their future. "The setting sun is boundless and great, but it's very close to dusk." Here Li Shangyin, a poet of the Tang dynasty, expresses the pity of not being able to hold on to such beauty, a vivid reflection of the experience of aging.

A lot of elderly people are materially comfortable but feel empty inside. An intense sense of loneliness coupled with not knowing how to spend your time can sink you into despair. As you age, your body's energy gradually declines, very few teeth remain, tasty food can't be digested, eyesight dims until you can't see distant or fine objects, and you can't hear even loud voices. You also become forgetful, perplexed, and fed up with the suffering of aging and various diseases.

The elderly actually have a great deal of time and freedom, but often they can't find anything that takes their interest, and apart from the occasional phone call, their children rarely keep them company or show concern, being busy with their own lives. Consequently, the elderly often feel gloomy and depressed, their tempers more unstable, and their moods sadder.

In Japan, about ten thousand elderly people commit suicide every year. In the U.S., the figure is nearly fifty thousand. Dharma practice is a good choice for the elderly. Because of their life experience, they aren't easily lured by elusive desires, so once introduced to the Dharma, it often resonates with them more than it does with young people. In Tibet, the elderly make themselves busy repeating the mantra of Avalokiteshvara, circumambulating stupas, and offering butter lamps, so much so that they rarely feel unbearable emptiness but instead complain that there's not enough time.

There's a saying: "Dharma study keeps children from being naughty and the elderly from dementia." If older people dive into the Dharma, they can accumulate merit for their next life, they won't feel so lonely in their old age, and more importantly, they will develop wisdom and possibly obtain liberation.

There's a story in the *Collection of the Sages of the Pure Land* that illustrates just how powerful Dharma practice can be. Once, an old grandmother in Hangzhou went to ask the monk Dao Yuan at the Xiao Ci Temple, "What practice can free me from the ocean of suffering in this very life?"

The monk told her, "No practice transcends repeating the Buddha's name. It's not difficult to repeat the Buddha's name, but to stay the course certainly is. Perseverance is not necessarily difficult, but to be single-minded is. If you can repeat the Buddha's name with absorption and with sincere aspiration, the Buddha is bound to meet you and guide you from the ocean of suffering at your death."

Hearing this, the old woman happily bowed and left. Back home, she handed over the housework to her daughter-in-law and other family members, cleaned up a room for herself, and practiced every day, repeating the Buddha's name.

Several years later, the old woman went to the monk again. "Thank you for your instruction. I gave up all the housework and have constantly repeated the Buddha's name. I can continue without interruption, but I find it difficult to be single-minded. Please give me your advice."

The monk said, "Although you gave up all the housework, your attachment to your children and grandchildren remains. Without overcoming this, how can you be single-minded?"

The woman agreed, "You're absolutely right! I can control my body but failed to control my mind. I will try to let go of everything." Back home again, she repeated the Buddha's name with great awareness, slowly severing her attachments.

Soon she came to be referred to as "Carefree." Several years passed in this way, and then she went to see the monk again and said, "You didn't lie to me. Your disciple is going to the pure land in a few days." Several days later, she passed away without any sign of illness. Her room was filled with a rare fragrance, and there were auspicious signs.

Birth, Old Age, Sickness, and Death
Are Just a Part of Cyclic Existence

Nobody is happy to grow old, so all sorts of methods have emerged to stay youthful. Mountains don't stay green, however, and wrinkles deepen every day. Nobody can hold back the force of impermanence.

In old age, the flesh and blood in the body deteriorate. The muscle between the bones and skin shrinks, making the bones more distinct and the joints and cheekbones protrude. Many people agonize over these changes, but it's not worth being upset about. In autumn, no matter how well you have watered the flowers, they still wither. Aging is no different. This is a natural law, so why not simply accept it?

I heard about a sixty-two-year-old woman who wanted to look younger. She insisted on having a series of operations, including a facelift and breast enhancement. Unfortunately, she died during one of the procedures. To make matters worse, before the surgery, she told her husband that she was having a minor thousand-dollar operation, but in fact it cost almost forty thousand dollars! Many people are stuck in this mindset and don't understand the laws of birth, old age, sickness, and death. They blindly engage in meaningless things and don't understand that once aging pays a visit, it's useless to invest in a strategy to escape it.

Five conditions of old age are described in the *Yogachara Stages*, an important Buddhist work. First, vigor declines and the youthful gloss of the body and face disappears. Second, energy declines, and though you were energetic in the past, you become frail and vulnerable. Third, the sense faculties decline—the eyes, ears, nose, and tongue deteriorate each day. Fourth, enjoyment declines, and although you could once enjoy all kinds of sensory pleasures, in old age, those desires can't be satisfied. Fifth, your lifespan declines, since the life you have remaining decreases with each moment. Nobody can escape these five destinies if they live long enough. Nobody can transcend the laws of birth, aging, sickness, and death.

Unable to bear the suffering of growing old, some people wish to die early. But when death actually arrives, they are frightened and want to avoid it. There is a world of difference between how a true practitioner faces growing old and how ordinary people face it. Practitioners can even use aging to guide people toward virtue.

I heard a story about an old Japanese Zen master whose relatives came to visit. They explained that his nephew lacked ambition, led a life of debauchery, and hadn't engaged in honest work. They asked if the master could teach him some Dharma, and the master agreed to pay him a visit.

When the Zen master arrived in his hometown, his nephew suspected that the visit was for disciplining him. But he still offered his uncle dinner and invited him to stay overnight. To his surprise, the master didn't make any strict remarks, as if he hadn't intended anything.

The next day, when he was leaving, the master asked his nephew, "As I'm old with shaking hands, would you help me tie my shoelaces?" His nephew was glad to do it. The master said, "Thank you! Being old is useless—you can't even tie your shoelaces. Take good care of yourself! Be a good person and make a good foundation for your career while you're still young." Then the master left, having said nothing about his nephew's bad behavior. From that day on, his nephew regretted his past behavior and sought a better life for himself.

Facing aging unperturbed is the best thing you can do. It's no use insisting on being like a forty-year-old when you're eighty. Sakya Pandita remarked, "People all envy long life but fear aging. To fear aging while wishing for a long life is the view of fools." It's easy to say that you will accept your old age, but when it arrives, how will you really react? How you face it depends on whether you have achieved any realization. If you do gain some level of realization, then aging is just part of the practice.

Don't Leave Practice till the Last Minute

If you start practicing at twenty, you may be able to secure the happiness of future lives by eighty. If, however, you live your life in confusion and want to start a fresh page at the end of your life, you will have no energy, time, or opportunities.

I heard a story about two brothers who lived on the eightieth floor of a high-rise apartment building. One time they arrived home in the middle of the night only to find that the elevator was out of service. Feeling energetic, they agreed to climb the stairs.

By the time they reached the twentieth floor, they were already tired. The older brother said, "Our bags are too heavy. Let's leave them here and get them tomorrow." Leaving their backpacks, they resumed climbing and it was much easier.

On the fortieth floor, the younger brother began to complain. "You had seen the out-of-service notice. Why didn't you say something? We could have come back earlier and avoided this!"

The older brother replied, "I forgot. What am I supposed to do?" They kept on arguing as they climbed.

By the time they made it to the sixtieth floor, they were worn out. Although they were still angry with each other, they had no energy to fight anymore. After a short rest, they continued to climb.

Finally, they reached the eightieth floor, totally exhausted. After catching their breath, they went to open the door, reaching into their pockets for their keys. They both discovered that they had left their keys with their bags on the twentieth floor! They had no choice but to sleep in the hall.

This story represents the different stages of human life. At twenty, your life is relatively easy and there's usually not too much stress. At forty, resentment and numerous complaints emerge concerning many aspects of your work and family. At sixty, although you are discontent, you don't have the energy to complain. At eighty, when approaching death and looking back on your life, it feels as though you have achieved nothing.

Also, at eighty you may feel like you left behind a vital key for your afterlife when you were twenty. If you had started practicing Buddhism then, you might have been able to attain some degree of realization. That said, we can encourage ourselves with this story. Although it's best to start practicing virtue when young, even if your conditions were not so fortunate, it's never too late to start practicing. This is certainly better than waiting until the time of death and having only regret!

8

Why Is Life Difficult?

A contented mind is one thing
that money cannot buy.

The Difficulty of Facing Impermanence

Everyone will eventually die. It's inescapable. From birth onward, we approach death day by day. Our lifespan is like a leaky pool to which water is never added—the level just keeps falling. The Lord of Death comes closer to us moment by moment, just like a shadow in the setting sun. None of us is certain when and where we will die; we can't even be sure we will not die tomorrow or even tonight. Never making an appointment, the Lord of Death pays a visit and takes our life right there and then. That's why the *Kshitigarbha Sutra* says, "The devil of impermanence always arrives unexpectedly."

In the *Sutra in Forty-Two Chapters*, the Buddha asks his disciples, "How short is a life?"

Some of his listeners say, "A couple of days." Others say, "The duration of a meal." The Buddha shakes his head.

Then someone says, "Life is the span between breaths."

The Buddha nods and says, "Yes."

This reminds us that life is extremely fragile. Without an unexpected natural disaster, your house can remain in good condition for decades. Our life, however, can't be guaranteed for even a few years, let alone decades. In Nagarjuna's *Letter to a Friend*, it says that once we fall asleep tonight, none of us can guarantee that we will wake up tomorrow.

The biggest problem people face is that they ignore impermanence. Naively thinking death won't arrive soon, they spend every day making plans for the following decades. It doesn't occur to them to think, "The path to death doesn't discriminate between the old and the young." The arrival of death is not as distant or uncertain as we want to believe. Exactly how and when death will arrive is always unknown. Who knows which will come first—death or tomorrow?

Some people may think, "Since death is everyone's destiny sooner or later, why fear it?" Emboldening yourself with this line of thinking is just self-deception. No one else's death is nearly as frightening as your own. If you really want to take responsibility for yourself, let go of attachment to this life and prepare for the afterlife. Most people turn a blind eye to death and avoid talking about it. Even though they understand that death is their only option in the end, they neglect it, try by all means to forget about it, and desperately cling to everything in this life without the slightest thought of what comes after it. They are just like the ostrich that buries its head in the sand when in danger. This is really ridiculous!

I am reminded of the Chan master Zhuang Yuan's *Poem Wakening the World*:

> Desperately chasing goals in haste and hurry,
> weathering coldness and warmth in fall and spring,
> keeping a household from dawn to dusk,
> hair whitening in confusion and dizziness:
>
> When will right and wrong be resolved?
> How long will it take to pacify afflictive emotions?
> A clear and obvious path is presented,
> but hundreds and thousands won't follow.

Eighty Percent of Suffering
Is Related to Money

Eighty percent of happiness has nothing to do with money, while eighty percent of suffering is related to money. So what is the Buddhist view on money? It is neither virtuous nor vile, neither pretty nor ugly. It can bring people suffering or happiness depending on how it's used.

A Tang-dynasty politician and author named Zhang Yue composed a short essay called the *Money Herb*. Through the metaphor of herbs, it explains that money is not a good or bad thing. If used well, it can benefit you and others and save lives, just like medicinal herbs. If used unwisely, it can harm you and others and take lives, just as herbs used wrongly can act as poisons. It's a pity how many people don't use it properly.

Patrul Rinpoche said, "A loaf of tea will bring you a loaf of tea's worth of suffering. A horse will bring you a horse's worth of suffering." In other words, the higher the value of the thing, the greater the suffering.

In the *Great Heap of Jewels Sutra*, the Buddha says:

> Wealth is like an illusion and a dream,
> but foolish sentient beings are duped by it.
> Gained in an instant and lost the next moment,
> how can the wise care for it?

There was a lay practitioner in the Tang dynasty named Pang Yun. Once, he loaded a ship with gold, silver, and all types of fine and soft goods and threw them all away into the Xiang River. When asked why he did it, Pang Yun sang this verse:

> The world attaches importance to money,
> yet I love stillness, even just for a moment.

Money usually disturbs your mind,
but stillness brings the suchness of all phenomena.

Of course, following this example or even seeing the illusoriness of money is unrealistic for most of us. That's why the Buddha said in the sutras that it's okay to accumulate wealth if it's through proper means. For instance, both the *Connected Discourses* and the *Virtuous Birth Son Sutra* say that our income should be divided into four shares: one for food and clothing, two for investment and profit, and the last as savings for unexpected times.

The Buddha didn't ask people to give up all their wealth. We can't just eat earth like earthworms. Especially for householders, without earning money to keep a family, there's no way to survive. This doesn't mean that we should worship money. Money isn't all powerful. People often say, "Money can buy you a house but not warmth, medicine but not health, books but not wisdom, a bed but not sleep."

It's a shame that so many people treat their money as the master and themselves as the servants. They have a house but still want another; they have a car but still want another. They exhaust their lives to get these unnecessary things and miss the happiness they could have had.

Mind Training Is an Art

No phenomenon in this world is not an illusory appearance projected by the mind. Unfortunately, most beings believe all phenomena are real and cling wrongly to their existence, thus inviting endless suffering.

How can this be so? The power of the mind is inconceivable—it can make any possible thing impossible and any impossible thing possible. We have trained our minds for such a long time in the belief that phenomena are real that the belief in this reality is second nature.

There's a saying, "Anything in the world can be achieved through training." Think about dancers: in the beginning they can't perform any movements, but through gradual training, they can dance wonderfully. In the sutras, the Buddha says:

> Therefore, whether it's real or unreal,
> through long-term training,
> that thought will arise without effort
> when the power of familiarization is perfected.

There are countless examples to support this statement. In one medical school, a professor gave every student in his class a pill and told them that it would increase their blood pressure. Not long after they took the pill, their blood pressure was examined, and it had indeed increased. Yet the pill was actually candy.

In another case a patient went to see his doctor because he had a cold. He had an x-ray and was diagnosed with lung cancer. After hearing the news, his condition worsened to the point where he could barely get out of bed. A week later, the hospital called him and apologized for their mistake. They told him that after reexamining the x-ray, they had found that he only had an infection and didn't have lung cancer. He felt better right away!

I had a similar experience. Once, I had a very bad cough for a long time. Our local doctor diagnosed it as pneumonia and told me there were serious problems with my lungs. That afternoon, my lungs felt terrible, and I started to think that not only did I have pneumonia like the doctor said, but maybe even lung cancer. Later I had an examination in a big city hospital, and they found nothing wrong with my lungs. I immediately felt better!

So you can see that the power of the mind is immense. That's why the Buddha exhorted us with great loving-kindness and compassion to "Maintain the view of the dharmadhatu, the ultimate expanse, that everything is only the work of the mind" and stressed that "Any appearance is illusory."

If you understand this, it really helps to lessen your suffering. If you think when encountering frustration or unhappiness, "All this is the work of mind. Without attachment it would not be like this," then what is at first unbearable can become insignificant.

Suffering and Happiness Depend on the Mind

What is the basis of suffering and happiness? Is it external objects or the mind? It is not a question most people even ask. Nowadays, many rich people live in luxurious mansions but suffer from incurable insomnia. In order to be promoted, those in positions of power smile forced smiles, are constantly restless, and have little joy in their life. This should be enough to prove that suffering and happiness depend on the mind and not on external circumstances like power or wealth.

If suffering and happiness truly inhered in external objects, then the same object should arouse the same feeling in everyone. We can see that this is not the case. Take the example of feces. Even just the smell of it can cause people to vomit, but some pigs and dogs find it delicious. Or in the case of the human body, Buddhists who practice visualizing it as undesirable may come to see it as a stinking skin-wrapped corpse, while those with strong desire think it's a wonderland.

The conclusion has to be that there is no suffering or happiness inherent in external objects. Everything is determined by the mind. When the mind believes it's good, there's pleasure. When the mind believes it's bad, there's suffering.

Tao Yuanming, an ancient poet, led a reclusive life in the mountains. He once made an instrument without strings; it had the appearance of an instrument but made no sound. Nonetheless he always took great pleasure in playing it. Did his happiness come from the instrument or from his mind? Only when we understand the nature of mind or emptiness can genuine happiness be understood. No matter how diligently we pursue happiness, it's just like a rainbow and becomes more and more distant from us. As Shantideva says in the *Way of the Bodhisattva*:

Although those who don't understand the mind's mystery—
the great principle of the Dharma—
wish to find happiness and quell suffering, they wander aimlessly.

It's Hard to Be Satisfied

Mental contentment is the greatest wealth of all. Even if you're penniless, you can still be a genuinely wealthy person. Nagarjuna's *Letter to a Friend* says,

> The Buddha taught that among all riches,
> contentment is supreme. Therefore strive always
> to be content. A genuinely rich person
> is one who is content even without material wealth.

I remember a news report that said there was a billionaire in Wenzhou who didn't feel happy. Once, when he was walking out of a five-star hotel with his staff, a beggar asked him for some money. He impatiently gave him a dollar. The beggar appeared extremely happy, which shocked him. He thought to himself, "How can a dollar make a beggar so excited?" His daily income was thousands of dollars, but nothing really gave him any excitement.

He asked his staff to leave, telling them he wanted to take a walk. After everyone left, he went back to find the beggar and treated him to dinner in an obscure restaurant. The beggar told him that he felt happy and comfortable and had sound sleep for eight or nine hours every day. This made the billionaire feel quite sad because he suffered from insomnia. No matter how strong the sleeping pill, he couldn't get to sleep. During that conversation he realized that wealth can't necessarily bring you happiness.

Su Dongpo's attitude toward life is another good example. Early in his career when he was the governor of Hangzhou, he often spent time looking at West Lake, meditating in boats, and discussing new recipes with his friend the Chan master Fo Yin. Life was very agreeable.

Later he was demoted and was sent to work in the south. At that time, the south was a remote desert. In that miserable place he couldn't even get the ingredients for his recipes. But in spite of that he said, "With three hundred lychees a day, there's no reason not to live in Lingnan!" He experienced life as pleasant because he could have lychees every day.

Sometime later, he left the imperial service. Even though he no longer received tributes, he thought, "When it's time for the Double Ninth Festival, chrysanthemums bloom. When it's mid-autumn, the weather is cool and the moon is beautiful." Even without having much, he was content simply with the spring and autumn festivals.

Su Dongpo was the kind of person that could enjoy whatever happiness arose and also undergo whatever problems he encountered without complaint. Lin Yutang, the twentieth-century writer, called him "an incurable optimist." This optimism was actually because he had contentment and little desire.

In comparison, nowadays some people have abundant material wealth and a luxurious life, but they still have no experience of happiness and are instead always complaining and morose. For these people, no matter how comfortable the external conditions are, it makes no difference. They believe that having good food, nice clothing, and an impressive house is true happiness, but in fact this kind of happiness doesn't last. The longest-lasting happiness is to have a contented heart.

Wealth Is Like Drifting Autumn Clouds

If someone really understands the principle of impermanence, they won't have a strong attachment to wealth. Actually, the wealthy are a great illustration of impermanence. The number of billionaires in China dropped precipitously between 2008 and 2009 due to the economic collapse.

To take another example, at one time Gong Ruxin was the richest woman in Asia. She and her husband had built a real estate empire from scratch. In 1997, she was listed in Forbes magazine as having personal assets worth seven billion dollars, richer by far than the queen of England. Later her husband died, leaving her embroiled in a nine-year legal dispute with her father-in-law. She ultimately won the dispute, but it did her little good. She died from cancer just a year and a half later.

Stories like this underscore Mipham Rinpoche's observation that "The body is like bubbles in water; wealth is like the drifting autumn clouds." It's a shame that people are so attached to luxury, wealth, and status and that only a few really understand this point.

In the *Song Wakening the World*, Master Han Shan also says,

> The spring sun just saw the green willows;
> the autumn wind just saw the yellow chrysanthemums.
> Glory and luxury are a midnight's dream;
> wealth and nobility are a September frost.

Through the green of the willows in the spring and the yellow of the chrysanthemums in autumn, we can see the change from spring to fall. Likewise, luxury is like a wonderful dream in the middle of the night, from which we wake up too soon. Wealth and status are like the frost in

September that vanishes in an instant. So contemplate the instructions of great Buddhist masters and try your best to weaken attachment to external objects, especially money!

More Money Is Supposed to Reduce Desire, but It Doesn't

The root of happiness isn't the amount of wealth you possess but how much you've reduced your desire. When desire is decreased, even if you sleep on the floor, you still feel happy.

People rarely feel content when burning with desire. Those who live in a one-bedroom apartment wish to move to a house with five bedrooms and then ambitiously strive for mansions. Even when living in mansions, they wish that in the spring, just by pushing the window open, they could look out on the cherry blossoms of Kyoto. In summer, from their home, they want to enjoy the cool breezes of the Alps. In the fall, in their own garden, they wish to watch the moon reflected on Lake Geneva. In winter, they wish that simply by walking out their door they could step onto the soft sands of a Hawaiian beach.

Once, a son from a rich Chinese family entered a kung fu competition but was completely defeated. Back home, he vented his anger on one of the servants, laying ten slaps across his face. Afterward, he regretted his behavior and gave the servant ten gold coins as compensation. The servant was so elated that, once he got the gold coins, the sharp pain in his face vanished, and he said, "Please slap me some more! I can stand a few hundred, so long as it's one slap per coin!" At this the son got even more furious and beat him violently without giving him a penny.

Nowadays many people are just like this servant, willing to take any abuse for the sake of money. They become good at "practicing patience" and are willing to be humiliated like cattle. It's as if they believe that money is omnipotent and can fulfill their every desire. Just as Shakespeare writes:

What is here?
Gold? Yellow, glittering, precious gold? . . .
Much of this will make black white, foul fair,
wrong right, base noble, old young, coward valiant. . . .
This yellow slave
will knit and break religions, bless the accursed,
make the hoar leprosy adored, place thieves
and give them title knee and approbation
with senators on the bench. . . .

People worship money in today's world, believing it to be all powerful. They believe money can bring them all happiness and everything they wish for, not understanding that happiness is actually a state of mind—the contented mind. And a contented mind is one thing that money cannot buy.

Competition

Competition with others causes restlessness and keeps the majority of people in a state of anxiety. In an Olympic race, a Japanese swimmer won the gold medal. Second and third place were won by American and Russian swimmers, respectively. After the race, a journalist interviewing the Japanese winner asked, "In the lanes beside you were an American and a Russian—did you know that both of them had held the world record?"

He replied, "I didn't know."

"Did you know that the other swimmers were close behind you, and the Russian once overtook you?" The journalist asked again.

Shaking his head, he said, "I didn't know. I only wanted to swim fast. I didn't notice anyone following or ahead of me. I think it's enough just to give it my all."

From this we can understand that if we perform without fixating on what others are doing, we can achieve great things. If our mind is preoccupied with competition, we unwittingly try to imitate others rather than focusing on our own unique skills. By going forward with focused effort, not measuring our progress against others or worrying about what our peers are doing, we can obtain our own genuine success.

Transforming Jealousy into Rejoicing

Jealousy is a common state of mind but is very harmful. There is a story about jealousy in the *Compendium of Analogies Sutra*. Once, a brahman had a wife and a concubine. His wife didn't bear children while his concubine gave birth to a boy. Out of unbearable jealousy, the wife secretly pierced the boy's head with a needle, and he died soon afterward. The concubine was heartbroken. Finding out that it was the wife who killed her son, she took the eight precepts and dedicated the merit to being able to exact revenge.

Seven days later, the concubine died and took rebirth as the child of the wife seven or eight times. Each time, she would be born good-looking, lively, and intelligent but always died unexpectedly while still very little. The wife was grief-stricken and wept even more than the concubine had upon losing her son.

Later, a monk who was the emanation of an arhat told her the cause. The wife understood and requested precepts from the monk. He told her she could take precepts in the monastery the next day. Just as the wife arrived at the monastery gate, the concubine appeared before her as a venomous snake and blocked her way. The monk, seeing this, berated her, reconciled their animosity, and made them repent their past resentments.

There's only one thing jealousy is useful for—it makes for great literature! There is the famous example of Shakespeare's Othello, who, burning with jealousy out of suspicion over his wife's infidelity, ends up killing her and then even himself. This may only be a story, but how many people can pat themselves on the back and say that traces of Othello can't be found in them?

It's best to avoid jealousy as much as possible. When others are happy, try to be happy for them. If it's really too hard to rejoice, at least don't make vengeful aspirations, like the concubine. Jealous people may succeed in harming others, but in the end they harm themselves even more.

Wealth and Morality

When I was in school, the atmosphere was quite negative. Students were always comparing whose clothing looked better or was the highest grade or even whose food was more varied and expensive. It seemed these were the primary goals of their lives.

In the Jin dynasty, Wang Kai—the uncle of Emperor Wu—and Shi Cong competed over who had more luxury. Seeing Wang Kai washing pots with sugar water, Shi Cong used candles as firewood. When Wang Kai had twenty-kilometer roadside screens made out of purple ribbon, Shi Cong had twenty-five kilometer screens made out of brocade. Wang Kai painted his walls with red halloysite, so Wang Cong used Sichuan pepper.

Emperor Wu was secretly supporting Wang Kai and gave him a very rare two-foot piece of coral. When Wang Kai showed it off to Shi Cong, to his surprise, Shi Cong smashed it with an iron-scratching stick and laughed. "Don't worry," he said, "I'll compensate you for it." Then he asked his servants to bring out six or seven pieces of coral, each of them about three to four feet long, much better than Wang Kai's.

These days this kind of competition has become the fashion in China, even in remote areas. Every holiday, people compare whose clothes are best and whose jewelry is more beautiful. In big cities, the competition for wealth is even more drastic. Some of the behavior is really absurd.

The key to a good life lies in morality and knowledge. As long as you have these two, your life is good no matter how poor you are. For example, the Chan master Hui Lin wore the same pair of shoes for twenty years. The Chan master Tong Hui wore the same clothes, which were patched again and again, all year round. How different this is from people today who chase fashion constantly and change outfits several times a day.

An adage says, "It's easy to adapt to luxury after being thrifty but hard to do the reverse." If you live a thrifty life initially, when the conditions allow, it's easier to adapt to luxury. However, to go from living luxuriously to being thrifty is very difficult. Once misfortune visits a family, turning them destitute and penniless so that they have to fight for a living, they are extremely fragile, and some even commit suicide. The problem is that in their infatuation with material affluence, they have neglected their spiritual development.

People today really need introspection. If people put as much emphasis on morality and learning as they nowadays put on fashion and pleasure, they would be far better off. The most meaningful thing for people to do is to make a selfless contribution to society, help sentient beings without wishing for anything in return, and avoid blindly competing with others.

How Can You Achieve Failure?

Arrogance, if not checked, can make people ignorant and even shameless. A story illustrates this. Once, in India, there lived a king with two sons. Knowing there was little chance for him to become the king, the younger son decided to devote himself to meditation. His father gave permission, and the younger son left the palace, went to an uninhabited forest, and practiced single-mindedly.

Not long after, the king passed away, and shortly afterward the older prince also died. A kingdom can't run without a sovereign, and so after some discussion the ministers invited the younger prince back to the palace. Initially, the younger prince refused, but after repeated requests, he went back and was enthroned.

After his enthronement, consumed with his newfound power, he became very arrogant and lewd. To satisfy his lust, he decreed that any unmarried woman in the kingdom must give their virginity to the king. His ministers were appalled, but no matter what they said, the arrogant king would not listen and instead had any minister who challenged him killed. This grim situation persisted for a long time.

One day, a woman ran out naked in front of a crowd of men and then urinated in front of them standing up. They called her shameless, but she just said, "We are all women here, why is this shameful? You women can pee standing up, so why can't I?"

They protested, "We are men!"

The woman immediately refuted them, "No, you aren't. The king is the only man in this kingdom. Otherwise, how could you stand to let your wives, sisters, and daughters be insulted? The behavior of the king is more shameful than mine. Why do you tolerate his but not mine?"

Her actions and remarks were enough to instigate the subjects, who had been driven beyond the limits of patience long before, to rush into the palace and depose the libidinous tyrant.

If you're arrogant and think you're superior to others, it's as though your body is covered by a raincoat—no water can touch you. Once you become arrogant, you are unable to gain more merit, and the merit you have cannot be enhanced. As the old Tibetan sayings go, "The water of merit can't stay atop the hill of arrogance" and "Merit's tender shoots can't sprout from the iron ball of arrogance."

Wise people have no need for arrogance, and unwise people only humiliate themselves with it. Mipham Rinpoche said,

> What need does a great man have for arrogance?
> Without pride, he becomes even greater.
> What use is arrogance to the inferior?
> With pride, they become even worse.

We should rid ourselves of arrogance and be willing to become the servants of sentient beings.

Wasting Others' Time
Is Like Robbery and Murder

People who don't value time enjoy chattering with others, whereas those who genuinely understand the impermanence of life and the rarity of human existence would rather give away money than waste a moment.

It's said, "Time flies like an arrow and never comes back." The decades between gaining a human body—with its freedom and advantages—and death slip away quickly. There's a Chinese saying: "A foot of jade is not so precious, while a little time is as precious as gold." For practitioners, time is even more essential than it is for others.

Once, before becoming Buddha Shakyamuni, the Buddha was born as a brahman who practiced in solitude. Impressed, the god Indra wanted to bestow on him some supernatural power. The brahman responded, "I have no desires. If you'd like to give me something, please grant me the gift of not being visited by you and save me the distraction." For a genuine practitioner, the greatest kindness is not to disturb them.

A lay practitioner once told me his greatest fear was someone coming by or calling, since it really wasted time. A fellow teacher of mine also told me, "I fear others chatting endlessly at my place under the pretext of stopping by for some serious matter, so instead I'll walk a long way to them so that I can leave once our discussion is finished and not waste any time."

Lama Nagongpa said, "Instead of talking about some plausible-seeming theory, people should read the biographies of the buddhas and bodhisattvas to learn how they have practiced the path from beginning to end. Only in this way will they be undeceived!"

In his *Talks on Literature*, the scholar Lu Xun said, "Time is life. Wasting others' time without a reason is like robbery and murder." So even if you can't practice yourself, make sure you don't rob other practitioners of their life's wealth!

Superpowers Are Not the Goal of Dharma Practice

Some practitioners become preoccupied with obtaining certain extraordinary abilities like clairvoyance and visions of deities. People like to crow about "such and such brings the divine eye" or "so and so has seen Avalokiteshvara." Some study the Dharma in pursuit of these things, not understanding that they don't lead to liberation and may even lead to the path of demons instead!

Once, Geshe Dromtönpa and four yogis of Radreng Monastery went to practice in retreat. One day the sun was high in the sky and it was time for lunch, but they had no food. Hungry, they started discussing what to do. Gönpawa said, "I will eat the food that is presently being carried up the mountain."

Just then a benefactor arrived with some delicious vegetarian food, and they all had a real feast. Geshe Dromtönpa always hid his virtues and wasn't pleased with this display of supernatural ability. He scolded Gönpawa: "Give up your false pride!" Unless there is a real need, great meditators don't display their supernatural abilities and only guide sentient beings by expounding the Dharma.

Nowadays, some practitioners like to talk nonsense all day, boasting about their dreams, spiritual experiences, and telepathy. Actually, these things are not important. If you become less selfish and more altruistic through practice, that is the most amazing superpower of all!

Great Fortune Belongs to Those
with an Altruistic Mind

What is the purpose of obtaining buddhahood? A lot of people love talking about buddhahood and long for it, but their motivation is not clear. Patrul Rinpoche said that the reason for becoming a buddha is to benefit sentient beings. It's not for your own happiness. Studying the Dharma is for becoming a buddha, and becoming a buddha is for benefitting everyone.

Atisha's *Questions and Answers for the Disciples* says, "Everything else is inferior to helping others. Every other thing in this world is insignificant; only helping others is peerless. This is also what brings great joy to the buddhas."

The *Avatamsaka Sutra* says, "All the buddhas are pleased if you please sentient beings."

There was a famous practitioner in Tibet called Ra Lotsawa. Once, when he was planning to enter a long solitary retreat to abide in stable meditative concentration, a deity appeared to him and said, "Even if you can abide in the peace of the concentration of cessation for hundreds and thousands of eons, the merit is not as great as that of sowing the seed of liberation for one single sentient being." Having received this instruction, he wandered around liberating beings from then on.

Helping others is the most significant practice. Even if you can't help sentient beings through action, Shantideva teaches that even the merit of wishing to benefit them far surpasses that of making offerings to all the buddhas.

The *Supreme Moon Lady Sutra* also says, "If even the mere thought of helping others brings infinite benefits, what need is there to mention the benefits of taking action?" Yet some people are so shortsighted that they completely give up the desire to benefit others and instead focus on their own short-term interests. This is just like the child in a story from the sutras who gave up a wish-granting jewel for some candy. How foolish! These days a lot of people are just like him—not realizing the value of altruism, they abandon the most precious thing for trivial gains. The *Way of the Bodhisattva* says, "Whatever joy there is in this world comes from wishing for the happiness of others, and whatever suffering there is in this world is caused by wanting happiness for yourself." So even if you wish to gain happiness and avoid suffering just for yourself, at least do so with an altruistic mind!

Once, there was a kind couple who lost their jobs, so they opened a small restaurant. Right from the beginning they won a lot of regular customers simply due to their kindness. Every day beggars would come to beg for food, and the couple always gave them fresh food instead of leftovers. They did these virtuous deeds out of the kindness of their hearts.

One night, the area where the restaurant was caught fire. The same beggars who always begged from them risked their lives to move everything out of the restaurant. When the fire engine finally arrived, only their restaurant was saved in time, while the adjacent stores were destroyed.

This shows the importance of altruism and a good heart. It doesn't matter if you lack other things, but don't lack this. Without it, fortune may never arrive, and misfortune will already be on its way!

Not Wanting Anything in Return
Brings Great Returns

When the Buddha was still a bodhisattva, whenever Indra asked him why he gave away his body, property, kingship, wife, or children, he always replied, "Because I only want sentient beings to be happy, not for any other reason." We can't do what the Buddha did, but at least we can try our best to benefit sentient beings unconditionally. When you do this, don't wish for anything in return. Even though you don't expect anything, an unexpected harvest might appear because of the power of inconceivable causes and conditions.

I heard a story about a young college student who had no money and had to take a part-time job as a door-to-door salesman. One lunch time, he was very hungry and went to knock at a door to ask for some food. A girl opened the door. The college student felt a little bit embarrassed, but since he was already at the door, he said, "I'm very hungry, could you please give me some food?" The girl gave him a cup of water and some bread. He wolfed them down and asked her how much he had to pay. The girl answered that since they had so much food, there was no need to pay.

Many years later, the same girl was grown up and married. One day, she suddenly contracted a strange disease. She spent a lot of money to have an operation, but it didn't cure her. Someone suggested that she go see one especially skilled doctor. He admitted her to the hospital where he worked, and the results of her treatment were quite positive, so she stayed there for a long time. After she left the hospital, a bill arrived at her door. Having spent lots of money already and having almost nothing left, she dared not open the envelope. Finally, she plucked up her courage, took a deep breath, and looked inside. All it said was, "A cup of boiled water and some bread are enough to cover all your medical expenses." That doctor was the college student she had helped all those years ago.

Mencius said, "Those who love others will always be loved by others; those who respect others will always be respected by others." Life is just like the echoes in a valley—what comes back to you is what you send out. Because it is a natural law, karma is unerring. As long as you make effort, you're bound to reap the results, and the only question is whether it happens sooner or later.

Generosity Will Only Make You Richer

Many people don't understand karma. The cause of becoming wealthy is actually to give, but in order to become rich, they blindly take. The cause of a long life is to preserve the lives of others, but in order to live longer, they kill. This way they will end up poles apart from what they want. They don't want to suffer, but one experience of suffering arrives after another. They want happiness but destroy it like an enemy.

Once, in India, there was a very rich man named Punyadana, which means "the merit of giving." As his name suggests, he had a kind and compassionate nature and was ready to give away anything. Later people started calling him "The elder who gives to the lonely." This was because he gave away his family property seven times—always to lonely people. Once, he bought a piece of land for building a temple with enough gold to pave the entire grounds. But somehow the more he gave, the more successful he became, finally becoming one of the wealthiest men of his time.

In ancient China, during the late Spring and Autumn period, there was a similar man called Fan Yi. After helping King Yue to reconstruct the country, he resigned from all his official duties and went off in a boat to Lake Tai to do business. He had a knack for business, and in just a few years he had acquired a fortune in property. Rather than squandering it all on himself, he gave it all away to help the common people. Even so, after several years, he had again accumulated many properties. After his death, he came to be worshipped as a wealth god called Tao Zhu Gong and is still revered even today.

Who is the richest person in the world today? It's well known that Bill Gates, the founder of Microsoft, is one of the richest. He is also one of the greatest philanthropists. Every year he gives several billion dollars to charity. Li Ka Shing is currently the richest person in Asia. He is also devoted to charity and always sets aside a great deal of money to give away, helping the needy, sponsoring education, and so forth. So far he has donated one third of his family property to charity.

There's truth in what the Buddha said: "The cause of wealth is nothing other than practicing generosity." Only by giving and giving can you gain anything. If you never give, you will never gain anything.

Charity Is Heart, Not Money

When *charity* is mentioned, most people think it means giving money. Nowadays a lot of people think charity is just a hobby for rich people that has little to do with regular people like themselves, so they are indifferent to it.

It seems that these days even the rich aren't all that concerned with charity. Statistics from the China Charity Federation indicate that the wealthiest people in China possess more than 80 percent of the country's total wealth but less than 15 percent of them donate to charity. In sharp contrast, China is one of the largest consumers of luxury goods in the world.

But anyone with a kind heart can be charitable. Wishing someone to be happy is a kind of charity. In the *Nirvana Sutra*, the Buddha says, "If you have no hatred toward a sentient being but wish to give him or her happiness, this is called *charity*." It's a pity that a lot of people these days aren't aware of this type of charity. They stop at giving their money and neglect to give kindness to those whose hope is withering. But for someone living in fear or hopelessness, love and protection is the charity they may need the most.

Nonetheless, if it's really too difficult to help others emotionally or spiritually, even a small monetary donation can make a big difference. For instance, if ordinary people in cities were to donate the amount of money they might spend on a meal out or on a piece of brand-name clothing, it could be enough to sponsor a child's education in poorer parts of the world, a contribution that could change their entire life.

The charity of giving hope can start with you and me, right now. Rich people can give lots of material support, but for ordinary people, even a smile or a sincere greeting can make a real difference in the life of another.

9

Conversations with Khenpo Sodargye

*A person with jaundice may know
that the conch shell before him is white,
but still he can only see it as yellow.
Likewise, you may grasp many principles,
but it is only seeing directly
that allows you to cease clinging
and go beyond suffering.*

Relationships

I had a bad experience in a relationship that is still affecting my mood. How can I shake it off?

In Tibet, because of understanding the Buddhist view of impermanence, many young people are able to avoid a lot of pain when encountering problems in their relationships. The Han Chinese seem different. Normally, romantic love is based on possession. Once someone stops caring for you, or their affection changes and they are no longer "yours," you feel extremely distressed. Had your love for them been unconditional, then so long as they were well, you would feel happy. Whether you were together or not would not hurt you.

It has been said that love is a barrier young people can't easily cross. When you look back on your life in a few decades, however, you might laugh out loud. Your attachment to your lover's affection right now is like your clinging to your toys in childhood. Back then, if someone snatched your toy, you could cry until the sky collapsed and the earth split open. When you look back, you see how ridiculous that was.

Nowadays a lot of young people are helplessly trapped in the confusing net of relationships, and it makes them quite miserable. After some time, when you have more life experience, you will discover that this is nothing but the confusion of a particular time of life. Have confidence that as you grow older that kind of attachment will get weaker and weaker. Eventually it won't bother you at all.

I am Buddhist and I recognize that romantic love does not last, so I'm not so interested in falling in love. However, should I get married anyway, for the sake of marriage? Must love be the foundation of a marriage?

It's best for you to decide for yourself if you should get married. As a monk, it's not suitable for me to decide this! Whether you get married or fall in love, you might have a certain feeling, a certain expectation, at the beginning. Most young people really long for this kind of intense affection and believe that within it lies the key to happiness. But from the Buddhist point of view, once you are married, the key to your happiness is handed over to your partner, and from then on you're locked in. Of course, others may explain it differently. Older people have more experience with marriage, so you should ask some of them to answer this question.

Results

You see people who have done many good things but don't get good results. Then you see others who don't experience negative results even after they have done many bad things. Consequently, a lot of people believe it's just a spiritual cliché to say "What goes around comes around" or "Virtuous deeds bring good results, while harmful deeds lead to suffering." Why should we believe that karma really exists?

Karma exists and I have unshakable faith in it. But why then do virtuous deeds not always bring good results? And why do harmful deeds not always bring bad results? This is because regardless of the kind of karma we're talking about, it does not ripen right after it's created. A poor peasant might be destitute because he didn't plant any crops. Yet if he diligently farms, even though he won't be able to harvest his crops right away, he won't be so poor in the future. We can't say that it's pointless for him to cultivate crops even though he remains poor throughout the summer.

Time is required for our karma to ripen. Some karma matures in the very life it's committed, some is experienced in the next life, and some will take effect only after several lifetimes. So the law of karma is not as simple as all that. It is said that only buddhas can see the law of karma directly. And even as a concept, it requires systematic study to understand. Of course, it's rational for you to doubt it. It is good to investigate and ask questions. But karma is like going to school: you don't see the results right away. We see its truth over time.

A lot of people don't experience their regrets until the end of their life. What is our primary mission for this life? How can we have a meaningful life?

You're right that many people don't feel regret until they are at the end of their life. Some people are able to realize their mistakes in time, while some never get the chance. No matter what sort of person you are, if you really want to be responsible for yourself, you should learn to use this life in the right way.

There are several ways to do that. The best is to devote your entire life to creating good fortune for all sentient beings. The second-best option is to practice virtue and accumulate merit for yourself. The third is to avoid doing things that harm sentient beings. After all, all lives are precious. In these three ways, you can make up for a lot of past wrongs. You can also cleanse those wrongs through purification practices.

Who determines what happens in our life? Why do some people have happy lives while others are stressed and confused?

Some religions suggest that the pleasure and pain of life are bestowed by God. From the Buddhist point of view, your life is determined by you and not controlled by others. If there were a creator who determined who should be happy and who should suffer, it would be utterly unfair! If he let me suffer when I haven't done anything wrong or let me be happy every day when I haven't done anything good, I would have good cause to complain to him!

As Buddhists see it, a happy life is actually the result of virtuous deeds we have done in the past. Suffering is from our past nonvirtue. On first hearing this, some young people may not accept it, but it's essential to understand it. If you sow the seed of a poison, the fruit will be poisonous. Likewise, once you have committed a negative action, what ripens from it in the future will only be suffering, not happiness. So if you want to be happy in present and future lives, try by all means to avoid creating any negative karma, such as by taking the life of another being.

A great master in Tibetan Buddhism named Jigme Lingpa once gave a very good metaphor for karma: when an eagle flies, its shadow is invisible on the ground, but once it lands, its shadow quickly appears. Likewise, once a person performs a negative or positive action, it will follow him all the time. Though it may not be visible, once the causes and conditions mature, suffering or happiness will emerge right away.

Following the Conditions

What does "following the conditions" mean, and how can you put it into practice at school or in your career?

The phrase "following the conditions" is often used by those who practice Chan, and one now hears it being used more broadly in China. However, many people misunderstand it, thinking that "following the conditions" means to do nothing and just wait for fate to decide. If this is how you follow the conditions, you will miss a lot of opportunities. Genuinely following the conditions means making wholehearted effort and then letting go of the result.

For example, suppose you applied for a good job, putting in a lot of effort, but you still didn't get it. If you understood the concept of following the conditions, you wouldn't be so disappointed. The same applies to romantic relationships. If you placed great hope in one at the beginning but in the end it didn't work out, there's no need to be distraught, let alone to go to the extreme of thinking of killing yourself, as some people do.

It's impossible for everything to go smoothly. The outcome of anything is the result of complex causes and conditions. This isn't taught in school textbooks, but if you study Buddhist texts like the *Treasury of Abhidharma* or the *One Hundred Karmic Stories*, you will understand that success and failure in life is based not only on this life but also on actions we performed in past lives. If you understand this principle, it's easy for you to open your mind, let go, and face everything with a calm mind. This is what it means to follow the conditions.

I try to advise people to pray for blessings from the buddhas and bodhisattvas when in trouble, but they often scoff, saying, "If things work out, you say this is thanks to the blessings of the buddhas and bodhisattvas. If they don't, you say this is because of my negative karma. This is how Buddhism is: no matter the outcome, it always has a convenient explanation." I don't know how to refute this.

This is actually very simple to refute. When somebody commits a crime, their family looks for someone in a position of power to help. If he is released, they give credit to the person in the position of power, but if that person couldn't do anything, they think that the crime committed must be too serious. This is just like the blessings of the buddhas and bodhisattvas. The Buddha also explained in some scriptures that even he couldn't help some unfortunate sentient beings, so this is not a fault in Buddhism. The buddhas and bodhisattvas are not like a creator God. You still need to have created the karma to be able to receive their help.

It's said in Buddhism that people should be grateful and contented. However, as a college student, when I engage in a research project with my professor, I need the drive to keep diving deeper into the research. So on the one hand, I should be contented with how things already are, but on the other, I should strive for more. My question is how can I balance this contradiction?

The mind of contentment advocated in Buddhism is to decrease the desire for meaningless things; for instance, to be content with whatever money and enjoyment you may have. But in learning, we should never feel satisfied.

The great Tibetan master Sakya Pandita said in his collection of aphorisms:

> Just as the ocean is a great treasury of water
> that always welcomes the influx of rivers,
> the wise are treasuries of excellent qualities
> that always welcome precious good advice.

So you need never feel satisfied with learning, scientific research, or Dharma study. Don't think that after graduation from college, you need never study or read from then on. In fact, the more significant knowledge you gain, the more you'll be able to benefit yourself and others. So never feel satisfied with learning. This is the Buddhist view and also an indispensable attitude for exploring science.

Buddhist Theory

Would you please explain the difference between religious belief and superstition?

When you believe in any religion, whether Christianity, Islam, or Buddhism, if you don't understand its theories, it's very easy to become superstitious. For instance, some people go to monasteries to offer incense and pay homage to the buddhas in order to get a promotion or get rich. Although this can be counted as a sort of belief, if they have no idea what they have just done, or if they know nothing about the difference between buddhas and gods and instead use the Buddha as a tool to pray for money, then it is superstition.

In many monasteries, every day people perform prostrations in front of statues of the Buddha. I wouldn't say all of them are doing what I mentioned just now, but some people are tainted by superstition. Why? Because they don't even know why they are paying homage to the Buddha.

Genuine belief in Buddhism means using your wisdom. It means reading books by great masters in order to know that Buddha Shakyamuni has been to this world and that what he said, if applied correctly, can remove the suffering of oneself and others. This gives you sincere and unshakable faith in him from the depths of your heart. This is genuine belief. If you just believe in Buddhism on the surface but in reality are confused and don't understand its theories, then even if you're a Buddhist, it's still superstition.

Therefore offering incense and paying homage to buddhas is not necessarily the same as having genuine belief in Buddhism. Not understanding its benefits but only admiring its rituals is not genuine belief. Some people even pray for good fishing! When I went to southern China, I saw a lot

173

of people who went to offer incense in temples and pray to the buddhas before they went fishing so that they could catch more fish. This is just superstition.

It is said that the Dharma is as broad, boundless, and vast as the ocean. Could you summarize its meaning in three words?

Ethics (*shila*), meditation (*samadhi*), and wisdom (*prajna*)!

The Buddha explained that one would be punished for several eons for transgressing some ethical precepts. How should we understand this?

The precepts prescribed in Buddhism aren't designed to punish people. They may appear as a sort of restriction, but in fact they assist everyone to advance on the path to liberation. It's a bit like traffic lights. With them, drivers seem less free, but they do really protect the drivers. Similarly, through following the ethical guidelines for practicing virtue and abandoning nonvirtue, sentient beings can obtain liberation.

Is there any difference between Pure Land practice in Tibetan Buddhism and the Pure Land tradition in Chinese Buddhism?

The ultimate goals of Pure Land practice in Tibetan Buddhism and Chinese Buddhism are the same. You can say they are different routes leading to the same destination. Pure Land practice in Tibetan Buddhism teaches that through generating bodhichitta and repeatedly chanting the name of the Buddha Amitabha, one will finally take rebirth in his Pure Land of Great Bliss. The other major cause for being born in the Pure Land is the forty-eight great aspirations of the Buddha Amitabha. Therefore rebirth in the Pure Land can be accomplished through a combination of one's own effort and an external power. This is also advocated in Pure Land practice in Chinese Buddhism—what is emphasized, however, differs slightly among some lineage masters.

There are many mantras in Buddhism, such as the six-syllable mantra, the mantra of Vajrasattva, dharanis, and so on. The Buddha said every mantra has immense merit, so we should repeat some of them ten thousand times. My question is, what mantra should I choose in my practice?

I have had faith in mantra practice since I was little. The only difference is that now I don't have time to chant as many mantras as before. An old Tibetan saying goes, "When a child is able to say 'Mom,' he or she knows how to recite the mantra of Avalokiteshvara—*Om mani padme hum.*"

The Buddha expounded the merit of chanting mantras in various sutras and tantras. Regarding your choice of mantra, it depends on two things. First, if a mantra is closely connected with your lineage master or some practice you have been empowered with, then you can aspire to recite that mantra. Second, you can choose in accordance with your own situation.

For instance, if you have done a lot of negative things and feel you have heavy karmic debts, repeat the hundred-syllable mantra of Vajrasattva. If you would like to be wise and benefit sentient beings in every lifetime, you can recite the mantra of Manjushri. If you want to open your heart and act out of compassion, you can chant the mantra of Tara. Essentially, choose the mantra that is important for you and your situation.

Some Tibetan practitioners are indeed exceptional in repeating mantras. Not long ago, an old monk in our institute passed away. He had repeated 600 million mantras. Before my teacher Jigme Phuntsok Rinpoche passed away, he calculated all the mantras he had repeated in his life. The total of long and short mantras was 900 million, and while the short mantras can be as short as one or two syllables, such as *ah* or *hum*, the long mantras can be more than a hundred syllables. He passed on at age seventy-two, and until then he never stopped chanting mantras with his prayer beads in hand.

Tibetan practitioners usually never part from their prayer beads anytime or anywhere, whether on a bus, herding yaks, or farming crops. Many intellectuals and politicians in China can't do this because they would be criticized by their superiors. The situation is much better now, and if they chant mantras with a counter in hand, their superiors won't notice.

Setting aside the long-term merit of repeating mantras, it has temporary benefits as well. It can dispel conceptual thoughts and afflictive emotions and bring your mind to a calm and clear state.

I teach at a university in Germany. Tibetan Buddhism has found many adherents in the West. In Germany, its propagation was particularly successful in the 1980s. Why do people find it so easy to accept?

Tibetan Buddhism is indeed very attractive in Western countries. The other day I read that there are more than thirty Buddhist centers just in the Boston area in the U.S.

The main reason is that the Tibetan Buddhist teachings are very practical and don't just remain at a theoretical level; nor do they involve mere academic research. Instead, through the essential instructions of past great masters, they provide many practical methods for dispelling afflictive emotions, such as bodhichitta, or directly showing the nature of mind in the Great Perfection. The explanation is straightforward and makes sense, so it has spread very readily. The fact that it's easily accepted by people is due to its pure transmission, its supreme instructions, and its emphasis on listening, reflecting, and meditating.

In comparison, the Buddhism in some other places has become superficial. I have been asked many times, "Is making prostrations Buddhism? Is offering incense and paying homage to the buddhas Buddhism?" I reply that this is just a form of Buddhism, not its genuine tenets. Dharma study must be built on understanding the mind and transforming the mind. Being issued a certificate of refuge doesn't make you a Buddhist, just as shaving your head and wearing robes does not make you a monk or a nun.

Most people aren't fools—they only accept Tibetan Buddhism after they have benefited from it. Even Han Chinese college students in China have accepted it. This is because their study of Buddhism has produced benefits that they have observed for themselves. Otherwise, if it's just stories and doesn't actually make a difference, nobody needs it.

We have to face afflictive emotions and suffering all the time. Just as it's unlikely that anyone would refuse medicine that can cure their disease, it's unlikely that somebody would not take up Tibetan Buddhist practices once they have experienced their benefits.

Modern society is dominated by commerce and economics. What is your opinion on the tension between protecting the environment and increasing consumption?

I have thought a lot about this question. In our society, the daily rhythm is speeding up and the stress and pressure of work are increasing. At the same time, consumption has become increasingly high. In such circumstances, consumption and environmental protection are sometimes contradictory.

In contrast, Buddhism advocates that we avoid too much luxury, spending money like water, but that we also avoid going too far in the other direction, having no food and clothing like beggars that can't accomplish anything. We should be content with a basic standard of living and avoid indulging in desires or living for consumption. A lot of people buy stuff not out of need but out of a desire to compete with others. Seeing someone else's nice house, they want one too. Seeing someone else's nice car, they also feel the need to buy one just to keep up. Living in this way, they tire themselves out. It's much better to take things as they come and maintain your life in line with your fortune. That way you can be satisfied and avoid the great contradiction between consumption and environmental protection.

In addition, it's important to help sustain the environment. Conserve water and electricity and don't waste things carelessly. When I was in Singapore, I noticed they were doing very well with this. On a recent trip to Hong Kong, however, I saw almost all the lights in the high-rises were on until two or three o'clock in the morning. Maybe people were working at night, but I assume most people were sleeping, and it seemed a pity that electricity was being wasted for nothing. These issues are worth thinking about.

I'm a Buddhist, but I couldn't answer some questions raised by my friends. One friend said, "Buddhists spend so much time chanting. They believe chanting prayers can help others, but why not use that time to help others in practice? How does chanting prayers help others? Can just mouthing sounds have an effect?" How can I answer these questions?

You have learned some Dharma, but I believe you should dive deeper into it. That way you'll be able to answer questions from non-Buddhists. That's my advice.

Buddhism doesn't claim that everything can be solved by chanting prayers, just as medicine doesn't claim to be able to cure all diseases. Nonetheless, we shouldn't think that since medicine can't cure all diseases, there's no use in practicing it. Why not just go ahead and help sentient beings? Individual sentient beings' diseases are different. Some can be cured by medicine, some can't. Likewise, Buddhists spending a lot of time chanting can also help sentient beings in some ways.

I myself have had deep experiences of this. For instance, when I get sick or encounter some unfavorable condition, I always offer money to the Sangha for their prayers. People who don't believe in Buddhism may think this is superstitious. However, I have no doubt about it, because after having prayers chanted, many situations have been straightened out immediately. Just as medicines have the effect of curing diseases, through chanting prayers and relying on the power of the blessings of buddhas and bodhisattvas combined with pure motivation, an effect occurs. To understand completely why chanting has such power, you must delve into the sutras.

Animals are living, and so we say it is harmful to eat them. However, plants are also alive. If we eat them, is it as bad as eating animals?

The Buddha said in the *Nirvana Sutra*, "The buddha nature of sentient beings abides in the five aggregates. If you harm the five aggregates, it's called taking life." Therefore only life consisting of the five aggregates—

both body and consciousness—experiences genuine suffering. Animals have such life. Plants, though they respond to their external environment, don't have the five aggregates.

Some people believe that plants and animals are the same. This view is a big mistake. Even some Buddhists who have studied Dharma for a long time aren't clear on this. According to the Buddhist view, there's a huge difference between cutting grass and killing an ox. Killing an ox destroys the life of a sentient being, so it's an immense fault, whereas cutting grass is not taking a life in the Buddhist view.

Some may say, "Hasn't it been said in Buddhist texts that we shouldn't harm animals or plants?" This is true, but the meaning isn't the same. If you kill a person or deforest some land, neither are allowed by law, but the punishments are very different. Likewise, killing animals brings far more serious karmic consequences than cutting down a tree, which is a relatively minor misdeed.

This is why I lay such stress on Dharma study. A lot of people think, "It's a fault to eat meat, so it's a fault to eat vegetables, too." They don't distinguish the severity of the fault. Thinking in this way, it becomes equally wrong to steal gold and steal a needle. We need to develop our discrimination.

How can chanting the Heart Sutra *dispel unfavorable conditions?*

The *Heart Sutra* is the essence of emptiness. The root of fear, disaster, and unfavorable conditions is attachment to self and phenomena. With the realization of emptiness and the elimination of such attachments, there's no room for the malevolence of any demon, whether external or internal. The *Heart Sutra* teaches the most supreme emptiness of the perfection of wisdom. Through the might of emptiness and the blessings of the *Heart Sutra*, all the inner, outer, and secret unfavorable conditions are eliminated without a trace.

As a layperson, how do I harmonize worldly concerns and Buddhadharma?

Strictly speaking, there are a lot of contradictions between worldly concerns and the Dharma. In order to be a good practitioner, one must see through most worldly concerns. But on another level, a lay practitioner can also take Dharma practice into their daily life.

For example, you can have a daily practice where you try as much as you can to chant some mantras and do some visualization practices. At the same time, try to treat everyone you meet with loving-kindness and compassion no matter who they are or what circumstances you're in. Even in rough times, use Buddhist teachings to encourage yourself to take things lightly and without strong attachment. This way you should be able to harmonize these two.

At the moment there are some marvelous practitioners who have done their best to make worldly life and the Dharma compatible. On the one hand, they have taken care of their own practice. On the other hand, through the Buddhist teachings on loving-kindness and compassion, they have made an immense contribution to society.

Buddha taught this concept of emptiness, but great changes have taken place from ancient to modern times. How should we cultivate the view of emptiness today?

No matter what age it is, the Buddhist view of emptiness is not affected. If you're serious about cultivating the view of emptiness, I recommend that you study *Fundamental Wisdom of the Middle Way* by Nagarjuna, *Introduction to the Middle Way* by Chandrakirti, and *Four Hundred Verses of the Middle Way* by Aryadeva. After studying these three texts, you should have some understanding of the emptiness of all phenomena. Having this view as your starting point is helpful for facing the realities of life.

I often think that people these days are too busy. If only they had the chance to understand emptiness, then no matter what frustrations they encountered, they wouldn't need to struggle so desperately. The doctrine of emptiness has great blessing power, so I hope you can study it!

Ordinary people can't see past and future lives or heavens and hells. How can we be sure they really exist? How can we establish genuine faith in karma?

Establishing such perspectives isn't easy. This isn't just the case with Buddhist ideas of heavens and hells, but also in the field of astronomy, where there are objects that can't easily be perceived, such as black holes, other galaxies, and so forth. These aspects of the universe we do not generally see for ourselves; we rely on the discoveries and theories of astronomers. In the same way, the truths taught in Buddhism are completely based on the authority of the scriptures that record the teachings of the buddhas and bodhisattvas, because through their wisdom and meditation they can perceive what we can't.

Once, Stephen Hawking gave some lectures in Beijing. A lot of students couldn't understand his theories, and some even left before he finished. His theories were just too abstruse to be easily understood. He described how the universe isn't limited to the three-dimensional space we think of but has as many as eleven dimensions. This indicates that there are many things we can't see. So, as Buddhist logic on valid cognition also shows, the fact that we can't see something doesn't mean that it doesn't exist. Its existence can be deduced by reasoning.

I have often seen t-shirts printed with the Heart Sutra *on sale in monasteries popular with tourists. Can they be worn?*

I wouldn't recommend it. Clothes are used to cover our body and keep warm, while buddhas, bodhisattvas, sutras, and mantras are worthy of our homage because they lead us to liberation.

The Buddha said, "In the five hundred years of the degenerate age, I will emanate as words. Think that they are equivalent to me and revere them." Only those who don't understand karma dare wear the *Heart Sutra* as clothing. Many manufacturers make images of buddhas and bodhisattvas, the *Heart Sutra*, or mandalas and print them on clothing. Some people also offer me cups and penholders with the *Heart Sutra* on them.

I don't use them. If this trend continues, someday the *Heart Sutra* may even be printed on underwear!

But if we wear such clothes on the street, couldn't it plant virtuous seeds in those who see us?

If your motivation is pure, it may be possible. But there are so many different ways to plant virtuous seeds, and it seems to me that wearing those clothes has more disadvantages than benefits. It is better to choose another method.

Renouncing Worldly Concerns

Monastics don't drink alcohol or eat meat. So why did Chan master Ji Gong say, "Alcohol and meat pass through the intestines, while the Buddha remains in the heart"?

Right after this, Ji Gong said, "If worldly people imitate me, it's like entering the path of demons." Ji Gong was an accomplished master. He was able to keep the Buddha in his heart even after alcohol and meat passed through his intestines. Just like great masters of the past, he had reached a very high level of realization, such that meat and vegetables and alcohol and water were not different for him. However, as ordinary monastics or practitioners, we should never blindly imitate him.

Nowadays a lot of films and TV ads in China misinterpret this and take it out of context. They use the first part of the statement to justify drinking alcohol and eating meat. Many leaders who don't understand Dharma also like to quote this statement when they drink. I have a friend in Tibet who gets dead-drunk every day. When others try to dissuade him, he always defends himself with this quote. In fact, when he is falling over drunk, the only thing that could possibly remain in his heart must be alcohol and meat—certainly it's not the Buddha. So whether you're a monk, nun, or householder, it's best not to boast. Until you reach Ji Gong's level of realization, never use this quote as an excuse to commit negative actions.

Adversity

You said psychology is a subject that teaches people how to be happy. My major is psychology, but I don't feel happy at all. In my twenty years, my life has always been difficult. When I was a child my family split up. In my youth, I endured various hardships in junior and senior high school. Now I'm in my junior year of college. I'm longing so much to fall in love with somebody, but so far, I have pursued five girls, and all of them have rejected my advances.

I don't know if these count as "hardships," and when facing them, I have never thought or tried to commit suicide but have just tried to bear them with patience. However, I'm not happy, and my greatest confusion is that I don't know why I'm here in this world. Am I here just to suffer?

I know that according to Buddhist theory, this is karma. My suffering comes from the negative deeds I committed in past lives. However, how can I get some positive effect in this life to eliminate the negative causes?

You said psychology can't bring you happiness, but if you study the psychology of Carl Jung, and especially the psychology of the mind in Buddhism, you will definitely find a sense of happiness, albeit slowly. You said you have encountered all sorts of unfavorable experiences from childhood until now, but from what you have described, some may not be so bad. You may have neglected to see their positive sides.

As you mentioned, whatever you experience in life is related to karma. Because of the deeds of past lives, some efforts made now may come to nothing. For instance, some students perform well on a daily basis but fail their final exams. Some people have a very good character but are always misunderstood by others. Others have a wide social network but still can't launch a career. Karma is just like a giant web—vast, boundless, and pervasive. If you understand karmic theory, you should reflect carefully when you suffer and recognize it as the fruits of our past deeds. This way, you can purify the negative karma created in previous lives and not perpetuate it into the future.

Of course, the favorable and unfavorable conditions in life aren't fixed. As long as you adjust your state of mind, unfavorable conditions can turn into favorable ones. However, if your state of mind is not right, even favorable conditions can become unfavorable. For example, some people endure all sorts of bad experiences in childhood, but this miserable life strengthened their hearts and made them more compassionate. Some people, on the other hand, are spoiled as children and believe that things should come easily, so when they grow up, they can't bear the slightest inconvenience.

Therefore the trials of life aren't necessarily bad. If you view them as an opportunity to improve yourself, your life will become more valuable, and your future prospects will be brighter.

I have read many Buddhist stories, and they all teach us to be patient and tolerant when facing challenges and then to let go and decrease our attachment. My problem is—and maybe this is because of my poor self-cultivation—I just can't seem to do this. What should I do?

Letting go is not easy. Letting go isn't achieved just by telling yourself to let go. You have to understand the theory first and then through practice gradually let go. A patient with jaundice knows clearly that the conch in front of him is white, but before he is cured, he can only see it as yellow. Likewise, you may understand many principles, but this can't be counted as knowledge but only understanding of the words. Only with genuine understanding will you cling to nothing and not suffer.

When facing personal conflicts, I always end up forgiving others. Even so, I'm always misunderstood and even treated like an idiot by others, which really depresses me. How can I find the balance between forgiving others and not feeling depressed?

This is a very common problem. Even people following Confucianism and practicing good manners are teased by their teachers and classmates. In modern society, many people make light of goodness, and virtuous practices like forgiving others are not always appreciated. Nevertheless, we shouldn't abandon our goodness and tolerance.

Mipham Rinpoche said,

> Even if the entire earth becomes covered
> with vicious people doing malicious deeds,
> I will never change my noble conduct,
> like a lotus flower sprouting from the mud.

Even if others think you're foolish, you shouldn't feel ashamed. This is the only way that you or society can have hope for the future.

If someone keeps complaining about something and is very attached to his point of view, how can I make him let it go?

Some people always complain about their situation even when it isn't rational. Why? Because by focusing on others' faults, they don't have to look at their own. When something fails, they complain about others. When they are successful, though, they give all the credit to themselves. A lot of people have this habit, and it's very destructive.

It's much better to think the other way around. When you're successful at something, give the credit to others. When something fails, accept the blame as your own. As the famous Tibetan saying goes, "I should accept the blame and give the victory to others." This is a great way of thinking, and it's a worthy yardstick for our behavior. The reason a lot of people are unhappy when relating to others is that they haven't understood this. Of course, it's not easy to put this into action, but even so, try to make effort in this direction.

In terms of helping this person to let go of his way of thinking, it's not as easy as just telling him. He must first understand the reality of the situation, and then through some practice, he might be able to let go. Only through examining it from different perspectives can we find it to be just as it is. Then letting go is as easy as falling off a log.

Desire makes us vain and competitive to the point that we forget who we are and what we really need. How do we discover and see ourselves clearly?

You're right that modern people are often vain and aggressive. To keep your mind at peace in this kind of society, it's important to have the right beliefs. If not, you will blindly chase after money, and with endless desire, you will never be happy. A popular slogan at the moment is "give the people what they want." But the people can never be satisfied. Our minds are like bottomless pits that can never be filled up. In our daily life, as well as pursuing material wealth, we can't neglect our peace of mind. To realize peace of mind, the ultimate answer is found in the teachings of the Buddha.

It was through witnessing the suffering of sentient beings and wishing to find a solution that the Buddha gave up the householder's life and practiced in solitude until he finally obtained buddhahood. Through Dharma study, we also expect to reach buddhahood one day, but our mind is not as strong as the Buddha's. What should we do when facing suffering?

Suffering is a trigger for the mind of renunciation. When suffering turns into motivation for accomplishment, it's called taking suffering onto the path. This is very important for practitioners. In Tibetan Buddhism, a lot of great masters prefer not to have favorable conditions every day, because they believe that suffering will help them to make progress in their practice. As Mahayana practitioners, we shouldn't feel miserable like worldly people when encountering enemies or unfavorable conditions. We should feel happy, because this helps us greatly in our realization.

I broke a ligament five years ago, and it's painful even now. I haven't been able to work out since then. Several months ago, when I resumed working out, the same ligament broke again. Why is my body so weak? How should I deal with this?

First treat any disease or ailment with the help of a doctor. In addition, you can adjust your state of mind. I suffered from ankylosing spondylitis ten years ago. Many doctors told me that it was incurable and I would have to live with the pain for my entire life. At the same time, I had hepatitis and chronic gastritis. After reading my health report, a doctor said, "You're so unlucky! You have so many serious ailments."

I might have felt anguished if I hadn't studied the Dharma. However, since I have studied Mahayana Buddhism, it really didn't get me down. I simply reflected that my body would perish sooner or later no matter how well it was maintained, and that no matter how many days I had to live, I would do something meaningful with them.

After doctors read my report and told me that I might not live very long, I found a place to stay in Xiamen and translated the *Great Biography of Buddha Shakyamuni* in solitude. While I was translating, I was afraid that I might leave this world in the middle of doing it. I felt that I would not have any regrets if only I could finish it well. Nevertheless, I somehow recovered from all of these diseases, and the symptoms have since disappeared.

When you are ill, don't dwell on how miserable you are or take it too seriously. In fact, it's okay to be sick or healthy. If my diseases can't be cured, I can think it's my karmic obscurations from previous lives and can practice taking the suffering of sentient beings upon me. With that state of mind, you can be happy no matter what happens, and sometimes you may be cured even without medicine. But if you're beyond a cure, it's not just you who will die. Everybody has to leave eventually; there's no choice. This is the way of cyclic existence.

What has been the greatest suffering in your life and how did you face it?

I was born in 1962, so I'm already more than fifty. I began elementary school very late, when I was fifteen. Before that I was illiterate and spent every day herding yaks. My younger brother was unwilling to go to school, and my parents were afraid of being fined for that. Without any other choice, they sent me as a substitute for my brother. Even now, my brother still likes to joke, "I was very kind to you. If it weren't for me, you would have had to herd yaks in the mountains your whole life and would have had no opportunity to become educated."

When I used to herd yaks, sometimes they were lost or eaten by wolves. When that happened, I dared not go home and was very upset. When I was in school, I didn't receive any awards. I also suffered greatly when I got into fights with other children. But from the time that I became a monk until now, I've devoted myself to Dharma study, continuously reading and meditating. During this period, I don't recall having suffered at all.

I was ordained in 1985. We had a class reunion at my old school in 2005. Among all the students, two of us had become monks. When everybody shared their experiences of the past twenty years, there were all kinds of suffering—of those who had gotten married, some had divorced or had lost their child or husband. So many of my female classmates wept while they were talking. However, the other monk and I really hadn't experienced any major suffering, and it's still this way now.

Personally, I relied on Jigme Phuntsok Rinpoche as my teacher to study, reflect, and meditate systematically, understand the emptiness of the Middle Way and the advantages of Mahayana Buddhism, and live in a relatively pure environment. I really can't remember anything painful. Although my father and some relatives died later, I didn't experience it as suffering. Therefore it isn't just words for me when I say that Buddhism is really powerful for dispelling suffering!

Refuge

What is the meaning of "taking refuge" in Buddhism?

Taking refuge is the threshold for becoming a Buddhist. Taking refuge begins with a ceremony in which one commits to turning to the Three Jewels—the Buddha, the Dharma, and the Sangha—as one's refuge in the face of suffering and relying on the instructions of the Buddha to guide one's life from then on. Buddhist refuge has different types, such as common, uncommon, and tantric. Taking refuge in Buddhism cannot be done under coercion but must be entered into freely.

Tibetan Buddhism puts great stress on relying on a teacher. Doesn't this contradict the Buddha's instruction to rely on the Dharma and not on individuals?

It's not contradictory. The teaching of the *four reliances* taught in the Buddhist sutras does tell us to rely on the Dharma and not on people. But while it's true that teachers appear as people and seem to be what shouldn't be relied on, this is not what the instruction really means.

Mipham Rinpoche composed a work called the *Sword of Wisdom*, which I have translated into Chinese. It gives a very explicit explanation of the four reliances. In fact, relying on the Dharma and not people refers to the process of practice. The goal is to rely on the content of the Dharma, such as practicing the mind of renunciation and developing bodhicitta, and not on the person delivering the teaching per se. Thus, if a rich, famous, and popular teacher gives teachings that are not in accordance with the sutras and commentaries, we should follow the sutras and commentaries.

But in order to genuinely "rely on the Dharma," we must first rely on a qualified teacher. This is a necessary foundation. Otherwise, it would be as the *Avatamsaka Sutra* says, "Without the guidance of a qualified teacher, no matter how wise you are, it's impossible to master the truth of the Dharma."

The object of refuge can be the teacher, who is the Three Jewels in one entity, or the Three Jewels themselves. We should understand Buddhism to be like a university. Without a guru, it's like a school without teachers. No matter how good the teachings are, not many people will be able to master them.

As disciples outside Tibet, we can't choose a guru after many years of observation, as Tibetan people do, but must accept the conditions we have. If the guru transmits the Dharma properly, disciples gain strong faith in that teacher. Sometimes, though, when some disciples find out that their guru lives in luxury, they lose faith. What should we do when facing such circumstances? How can we judge the manifestation of a guru?

I believe disciples in other places also have the conditions to observe a guru. You have time and other causes and conditions. If Tibetan people have it, why don't others have it? Nowadays, when they hear that a guru is in town, a lot of people immediately accept empowerments and teachings from this guru without any observation. This is reckless. When people choose a partner with whom they plan to live for their entire life, they don't just grab someone off the street. First they find out about his or her background and spend time observing his or her character.

Since seeking liberation life after life is more important than this, it goes without saying that it is indispensable to follow a guru. Therefore it's irrational for anyone not to follow one. From now on, try and observe a prospective guru just like Tibetan people do. Your guru is a highly qualified teacher if he devotes himself to propagating the Dharma and is not attached to luxury or wealth and instead views them as being like feces.

I met one guru who was offered a very good house in the city. I joked with him, "Now that you have a house and a car, you aren't any different from worldly people!"

He laughed and said, "To be honest, my attachment to that house isn't any more than to my yak-dung shed." I know him very well—he wasn't boasting. So for some gurus, no matter how wealthy they are, they aren't as greedy as worldly people. It doesn't matter to people like that how many mansions they have.

Some so-called gurus, however, lack any qualification and are even worse than ordinary people. They shamelessly seek personal gain, and none of their behavior has anything to do with propagating the Dharma. You should stay away from people like that. At present, there are a lot of great gurus in Chinese cities. They are providing an opportunity for you to take refuge and study the Dharma. Without them, many people would be trapped in cyclic existence forever. Unfortunately, there are also some bad gurus, and their conduct should be exposed.

This world has a mixture of good and bad people. It's essential to discriminate well!

I'm about to graduate and am under a lot of pressure to prepare for my final exams. Should I put all my energy into my studies or still devote part of my time to daily practice? Which one is more meaningful for my future?

It depends. You shouldn't get behind. You're about to face a great change in life, and after years of education, you have to enter society and give something back. For this reason, it's better not to compromise your studies due to Dharma study. Don't postpone your studies or finding a job to complete a fixed amount of practice. You can make it up later when conditions allow. And while you are studying, you can still remain vigilant about avoiding mental afflictions and negative actions.

Loving-Kindness and Compassion

When you dedicated merit to the earthquake and tsunami victims in Japan, you used the mantra Om mani padme hum. *What do these syllables really mean?*

The mantra *Om mani padme hum* consists of the six syllables of Avalokiteshvara. Its merit is inconceivable and is described in many scriptures. By reciting *Om mani padme hum* for the deceased, whatever suffering they are experiencing is transformed into happiness. When disasters take place frequently, if we pray to Avalokiteshvara and recite his mantra, disasters can be pacified to the greatest extent possible through its power. Many scriptures mention this point.

Because of the Internet, information is now shared more easily. Should we use the Internet in order to shed light on injustice and awaken people's sense of righteousness? Or should we devote ourselves to practice and realization so that we can purify our minds?

Things are completely different now in comparison with ancient times. Things are very different even in comparison with the last century! Once something is uploaded online, it can be seen by countless people. The power of the Internet is truly immense. So long as our practice is not harmed, we can share genuine and valuable knowledge with many people through the Internet. It's meaningful even if you can only help one person.

At the moment, a lot of people are confused and suffering without any direction in their lives. They hang out online to find a spiritual home, but often they don't find one and instead only meet negative teachers who quickly send them down wrong paths. In times like these, it's crucial to protect the wisdom and even the physical lives of others through the Internet.

Of course if you have no motivation to benefit others, it's another story. But if you do have positive motivation, and if you can maintain your own practice, try by all means to help sentient beings. Even if there's some impact on your practice, still put the benefit of sentient beings first.

There's a lot of negative information online. The external environment is also polluted beyond recognition by industrialization. In many places we no longer even have fresh air to breathe. Living in a world that is dirty inside and out, we are unhealthy, both physically and mentally. Therefore I really hope you will spread positive culture and helpful knowledge online.

Death

My friend has just been diagnosed with an incurable disease and won't live long. He has just received this news and is very sad and unable to accept it. I really want to help him, but I don't know what to do. How can I help him with the Dharma? How should he face his remaining days?

Most people feel grief when facing the last moments of their life. But truly each one of us could face death at any moment. Our bodies are very fragile, and nobody can guarantee that we won't have a fatal car accident tomorrow or die of cancer next year. You should therefore prepare for it mentally. Never waste your life. Seize the present moment and engage in things that are meaningful and benefit sentient beings. If you can do this, then whenever death arrives, you won't panic or feel regret.

Your friend might not study the Dharma, or even if he does, he might not really practice it, so he doesn't have impermanence in mind. It's not realistic for you to expect me to give some essential instruction that would enable him to instantly face death with courage. We have to get used to such ideas.

However, you can still try to tell him that death is not the final destination of life but the start of the next life. Our body is just a hotel—a temporary shelter—so there's no need to cling to it. When facing death, fear is useless. The most useful thing is to make good use of the time he has left to do virtuous deeds so that he will be better prepared for his next life. If he refuses to accept that and is not able to believe in Buddhism, you can quietly dedicate merit to him and even chant some names of buddhas in his ear when he dies. This can have some effect.

Thanks to the blessings of the Three Jewels, we can't exclude the possibility of some miracle. I know one college student who had cancer. She let go of everything and chanted the Buddha's name with a single-pointed mind in order to welcome death. In the end, her cancer disappeared miraculously. The power of the mind is sometimes a wonder.

But by and large, if we only start to study the Dharma when we're at death's door, it probably won't benefit us much. So I hope you take this as a lesson and prepare for death in advance. Throughout the ages, many Buddhists have died with serenity. How? They always contemplated, visualized, and meditated. It is like what we see with athletes. Only with good training off the playing field beforehand do they rise to the occasion in the heat of a match.

What should I do to prepare for death?

If you have some property, it's better to give it away. If there isn't time to do this, at least give it up mentally. In some essential practices of Buddha Amitabha, it's said that when we are dying and both the inner and outer appearances indicating death have occurred, and when it's certain that death is arriving, we shouldn't cling to property or anything else. If there isn't time to give everything away physically, we at least can think, "I have wandered in cyclic existence from beginningless time, and only in this life have I finally met the practice for being born in a pure land. I must give up attachment to relatives and property and take rebirth there!" This is the instruction from the great gurus.

At the time of death, it's very likely that we will cling to "my family," "my house," "my money," and so forth. If those kinds of thoughts come up, it's impossible to take rebirth in a pure land. Therefore we need to avoid clinging of all kinds. What we have learned now can be used at death or in the intermediate state. No matter what, remember these instructions as best you can and really put them into practice. This is vital!

Practice

Since I started studying the Dharma, people are always asking me, "Why do you study the Dharma? Can it bring you food?" I don't know how to answer them.

You can ask them, "Do people live in this world only to eat?"

But they could still be confused if I explain it in that way.

Don't worry. If you explain it to them with reason, they should understand. If they can't listen to reason, there's no solution. It's normal that some people don't understand us after we begin studying the Dharma. In spite of that, Dharma study will help us in the present life and in future lives. When others see how it has helped us, then it won't be so hard for them to accept it.

My father is not in good health and often has headaches, so my mother offers clean water in front of statues of the Buddha every morning and chants a secret mantra a couple of times. She asks my father to drink the water and he suddenly feels better. However, isn't it true that one shouldn't chant a secret mantra without the empowerment? Is it okay for my mother to do so?

It's better to chant a secret mantra after empowerment. However, if one doesn't have the oral transmission and initiation for various reasons, it can still have an effect, and it's not a great fault to chant it. At present, both in Tibetan and Han Chinese areas, many people don't have the transmissions, but they still have inner experience and gain blessings after chanting.

Have you ever doubted or wavered in your practice? How did you overcome it? Have you experienced realization?

I'm an ordinary person, but I have strong faith in Buddha Shakyamuni and irreversible certainty in the truth of cyclic existence. If someone told me that past and future lives don't exist, I have thousands of reasons to refute them. Anyone is free to say that Buddhism is no good, but it will not shake my conviction. This is not simple trust; it has been accumulated little by little over the past twenty years of listening, reflecting, and meditating on the Dharma. This solid faith is in my blood and can't easily melt away.

However, as an ordinary person, when I see good food and I'm hungry, my mind will still waver. I feel ashamed when that happens because I repeatedly teach emptiness to others, but I can't keep my words and conduct in accord with each other. Therefore, in terms of realization, I can't say that I have any, let alone enlightenment. I just have unwavering faith in the truth of Buddha's teachings.

You have said you read poems by Tagore and Shakespeare. Do you read poems by Tsangyang Gyatso, the Sixth Dalai Lama? What do you think of them?

I like Tsangyang Gyatso's poems very much. With simple language, he used the most provocative topics—relationships and love—to gradually guide us toward letting go. Second, having read the secret biography of Tsangyang Gyatso, I see that he was able to face reality with great freedom and ease in spite of his difficult circumstances. When facing all sorts of problems, he never blamed others or even fate; nor was he defeated by the pain. On the contrary, he composed great poems depicting the most subtle states of mind. Such noble sentiment is really worthy of praise. Tsangyang Gyatso's love songs actually have three levels of meaning: outer, inner, and secret. Most worldly people only understand the outer meaning and believe these poems are suitable only for householders. They don't realize that they also have profound import for practice as well.

Fate

I have just been introduced to Buddhism and so far only have learned about karma, being calm and rational, and accepting the past. However, I just graduated from college and need to fight to achieve my goals for the future, which is in tension with Buddhism as I understand it. Are these two contradictory? If not, how can I resolve them?

No matter what dream you're fighting for, you'll succeed more quickly if you are calm and rational. If you become angry and flustered and lose your calm, it's unlikely you will succeed in anything. So how can you be calm and rational? In Buddhism it's said that we should first examine our mind before taking action. If our mind is virtuous, then we can proceed, but if our mind is corrupt, it's better to stop. What is a corrupt mind? It means that your motivations for doing something are harmful to society or others. A state of mind like that is certainly not calm. Therefore, if you want to achieve your goals, head in the direction of helping others. Then these two are not contradictory.

Some people misunderstand the way Buddhism treats life as being completely passive, evasive, or against wishing for success in the present life. Of course, achieving success requires merit from past lives. Otherwise, no matter how hard you strive, you will fail. Some people always complain, "I work harder than other people. Why are others so successful while I'm still so unsuccessful?" This can only indicate that they didn't accumulate enough merit in their past lives. If they had accumulated more merit, then whatever they attempted to do now would be as they wished, and it would be very easy for them to succeed. Without understanding this, it's easy to blame others and feel that society is unfair.

The Sutra of the Foolish and the Wise *states the four extremes of impermanence: "Whatever comes together is impermanent and is bound to come apart. Whatever is stored up is impermanent and is bound to run out. Whatever is born is impermanent and is bound to die. Whatever rises up is impermanent and is bound to fall down." What is the importance of this verse for our daily lives?*

These are very important principles. They appear to be very simple, but if you understand their profound meaning, you will be able to cope with any kind of suffering. First, especially in relationships, people who are together today don't understand that they will part ways sooner or later. Second, they don't understand that whatever is stored up is bound to run out. When their hard-earned wealth runs out one day, they would rather die than live any longer. Third, they don't understand that whatever is born is bound to die. When a person close to them dies, or when they are informed that they have an incurable disease, they completely lose hope. Fourth, they don't understand that whatever rises up is bound to fall down. If they lose their high status, they find no meaning in living any longer. If you understand the four extremes of impermanence, then you can avoid experiencing the suffering that can result from these types of events.

Once, I attended a school graduation. The students were reluctant to leave, and many were crying. I told them, "Whatever comes together is impermanent and is bound to come apart. Whatever is stored up is impermanent and is bound to run out. Whatever is born is impermanent and is bound to die. Whatever rises up is impermanent and is bound to fall down." Without such understanding, a lot of young people can't bear their pain.

Patrul Rinpoche expounds the four extremes of impermanence in *Words of My Perfect Teacher*. If you're interested in learning more, I'm sure it would be very helpful for your life and your practice to study it.

I'm very indecisive, but I'm also afraid that if my mind strengthens and I become more decisive, I might become impulsive and hotheaded and bring negative influences on myself and others. How can I use wisdom to make good decisions?

The famous Tibetan scholar Sakya Pandita said, "The difference between the foolish and the wise is that fools only examine afterward." Before taking action, a wise person would calmly think, "What will be the consequences of doing this? Will there be a lot of unfavorable conditions in the process? What approach can make it work? How will the final result benefit society?" It's important to consider these questions. If you do, then you won't be indecisive or impulsive but will stay on the middle way.

Postscript

Do you feel any different after reading this book? After almost thirty years of study and diligent practice in Tibet, I always find the Dharma to be vaster and more diverse the more deeply I understand it. Every time I leaf through a Buddhist scripture, I reap a surprising reward.

At the moment, I'm deeply touched by the Buddha's wisdom regarding the emptiness of all phenomena and his compassion toward all sentient beings. I really wish to share this with you, and that wish is the origin of this book.

Of course, what is included here is just a drop in the ocean of Buddhist teachings. I have just expressed my sentiments with a couple of sips from this vast ocean in the hope that you can taste its sweetness.

If wisdom, virtue, and a pure mind arise in you thanks to this book, then you will have a rudder when sailing through the ups and downs of life. You will have confidence that "the journey through future lives will be very difficult, with huge waves, but still one day I will reach the other shore!"

About the Author

Khenpo Sodargye was born in Tibet in 1962 in what is today the Sichuan province of China. He spent his early years herding yaks, and after attending Garze Normal School, he entered Larung Gar Buddhist Institute in Serthar, becoming a monk under the great Jigme Phuntsok Rinpoche. He is now one of the leading scholars of that institute, the fastest-growing Buddhist monastery in China today. He has been especially effective at popularizing Tibetan Buddhism among Han Chinese students, with numerous bestselling books, and he regularly speaks at universities in Asia and the West.

What to Read Next from Wisdom Publications

HOW TO MEDITATE
A Practical Guide
Kathleen McDonald

"Jewels of wisdom and practical experience to inspire you."
—Richard Gere

LIVING AND DYING WITH CONFIDENCE
A Day-by-Day Guide
Anyen Rinpoche and Allison Choying Zangmo
Foreword by Kathleen Dowling Singh

"Anyen Rinpoche has skillfully woven the dharma teachings into these everyday contemplations on death which will be very beneficial especially for those in denial or dealing with loss."—Tenzin Palmo, founder of Dongyu Gatsal Ling Nunnery

LOSING THE CLOUDS, GAINING THE SKY
Buddhism and the Natural Mind
Doris Wolter

"An eclectic collection of writings on Dzogchen.... Includes seven pieces by Sogyal Rinpoche. The many voices gathered here demonstrate the wide range of styles with which individual teachers of the past century have expressed the Great Perfection."—*Buddhadharma*

VAJRASATTVA MEDITATION
An Illustrated Guide
Khenpo Yeshe Phuntsok

Walk step by step through the stages of this tantric ritual of purification with inspired commentary and full-color illustrations.

WHO ORDERED THIS TRUCKLOAD OF DUNG?
Inspiring Stories for Welcoming Life's Difficulties
Ajahn Brahm

"Ajahn Brahm is the Seinfeld of Buddhism."—Sumi Loundon Kim

About Wisdom Publications

Wisdom Publications is the leading publisher of classic and contemporary Buddhist books and practical works on mindfulness. To learn more about us or to explore our other books, please visit our website at wisdompubs.org or contact us at the address below.

Wisdom Publications
199 Elm Street
Somerville, MA 02144 USA

We are a 501(c)(3) organization, and donations in support of our mission are tax deductible.

Wisdom Publications is affiliated with the Foundation for the Preservation of the Mahayana Tradition (FPMT).